SPPU New Syllabus

Text Book of

INTRODUCTION TO HUMAN GEOGRAPHY

For

F.Y.B.Sc. Semester II

Paper IV

New Syllabus as per CBCS Pattern, June 2019

By

Dr. Jyotiram Chandrakant More

M. A. Ph.D. Geography

Head of Geography Department

Indian Jain Association's Arts, Science and Commerce College,

Wagholi, Pune

President Geography Study Committee,

Savitribai Phule Pune University,

Pune.

NIRALI PRAKASHAN

ADVANCEMENT OF KNOWLEDGE

N5045

Introduction to Human Geography **ISBN : 978-93-89825-35-0**

First Edition : February 2020

Published By:
NIRALI PRAKASHAN
Abhyudaya Pragati, 1312, Shivaji Nagar
Off J.M. Road, PUNE – 411005
Tel - (020) 25512336/37/39, Fax - (020) 25511379
Email : niralipune@pragationline.com

➢ DISTRIBUTION CENTRES

PUNE

Nirali Prakashan (For orders within Pune) : 119, Budhwar Peth, Jogeshwari Mandir Lane, Pune 411002, Maharashtra, Tel : (020) 2445 2044, Mobile : 9657703145
Email : niralilocal@pragationline.com

Nirali Prakashan (For orders outside Pune) : S. No. 28/27, Dhayari, Near Asian College Pune 411041
Tel : (020) 24690204; Mobile : 9657703143
Email : bookorder@pragationline.com

MUMBAI

Nirali Prakashan : 385, S.V.P. Road, Rasdhara Co-op. Hsg. Society Ltd., Girgaum, Mumbai 400004, Maharashtra;
Mobile : 9320129587 Tel : (022) 2385 6339 / 2386 9976,
Fax : (022) 2386 9976
Email : niralimumbai@pragationline.com

➢ DISTRIBUTION BRANCHES

JALGAON

Nirali Prakashan : 34, V. V. Golani Market, Navi Peth, Jalgaon 425001, Maharashtra, Tel : (0257) 222 0395, Mob : 94234 91860;
Email : niralijalgaon@pragationline.com

KOLHAPUR

Nirali Prakashan : New Mahadvar Road, Kedar Plaza, 1st Floor Opp. IDBI Bank, Kolhapur 416 012, Maharashtra. Mob : 9850046155;
Email : niralikolhapur@pragationline.com

NAGPUR

Nirali Prakashan : Above Maratha Mandir, Shop No. 3, First Floor, Rani Jhanshi Square, Sitabuldi, Nagpur 440012, Maharashtra
Tel : (0712) 254 7129;
Email : niralinagpur@pragationline.com

DELHI

Nirali Prakashan : 4593/15, Basement, Agarwal Lane, Ansari Road, Daryaganj Near Times of India Building, New Delhi 110002
Mob : 08505972553, Email : niralidelhi@pragationline.com

BENGALURU

Nirali Prakashan : Maitri Ground Floor, Jaya Apartments, No. 99, 6th Cross, 6th Main, Malleswaram, Bengaluru 560003, Karnataka;
Mob : 9449043034
Email: niralibangalore@pragationline.com

Other Branches : Hyderabad, Chennai

PREFACE

It gives me great pleasure to present the textbook of Human Geography to our FYBSc readers. This book has been designed as a standard text book on Human Geography.

This book covers the entire syllabus of FYBSc Semester II. New course of Savitribai Phule Pune University, Pune effective from June 2019 onwards. This book has been written to fulfill the basic concepts. Some of the features of the book are observation, perception, analysis, critical thinking and understand the relationship between Nature and Human society.

The book has been designed in four chapters. The basic knowledge behind this is to present the matter in a systematic way. First chapter deals with the basic concepts of Geography, Introduction of Human Geography and its importance. Second chapter deals with the Human Evolution and Races.

Third chapter is on Study of Indian Tribes. Fourth and last chapter of this book is on Human Culture.

Every effort has been made to provided accurate information on the subject. We are very grateful to our publisher ***Shri. Dineshbhai Furia*** and ***Jignesh Furia*** who showed all assistance in publication. We wish to acknowledge our deep gratitude to staff members Mr. Prasad Chintakandi, Mrs. Surekha M. Sannali, Mr. Ravindra Walodare who have helped in preparing this book. This book will prove useful to all students and teachers of the subjects.

Yours reviews and suggestions are always taken positively. Please send them to us.

Author

Dr. Jotiram Chandrakant More

❋ ❋ ❋

SYLLABUS

F.Y.BCs. : Semester – II

Introduction to Human Geography

1. Introduction to Human Geography

(a) Definitions and Meaning of Human Geography

(b) Branches of Human Geography

(c) Nature and Scope of Human Geography

(d) Contemporary Relevance of Human Geography

2. Human Evolution and Races

(a) Stages of Human Evolution

(b) Meaning and Definition of Human Race

(c) Bases of Human Race

(d) Griffith Taylor's Theory of Human Race

(e) Pure and Mixed Races

3. Study of Indian Tribes

(a) Regional Distribution of Tribes in India

(i) Bhil, (ii) Gond, (iii) Naga, Tribes in Maharashtra

4. Human Culture

(a) World Languages and their Distribution

(b) World's Major Religions and their Distribution

(c) Distribution of Language and Religions in India

❋ ❋ ❋

CONTENTS

❋ ❋ ❋

UNIT – 1

INTRODUCTION TO HUMAN GEOGRAPHY

SYNOPSIS

INTRODUCTION

Human Geography is the study of the interrelationship between people, place, and environment, and how these vary spatially and temporally across and between locations. Physical geography concentrates on spatial and environmental processes that shape the natural world and tend to draw on the natural and physical sciences for its scientific underpinnings and methods of investigation. Human geography concentrates on the spatial organization and processes shaping the lives and activities of people, and their interactions with places and nature.

Human geography is more allied with the social sciences and humanities, sharing their philosophical approaches and methods.

Human geography consists of a number of sub-disciplinary fields that focus on different elements of human activity and organization.

For example, cultural geography, economic geography, health geography, historical geography, political geography, population geography, rural geography, social geography, transport geography, and urban geography. What distinguishes human geography from other related disciplines, such as development, economics, politics, and sociology.

The application of a set of core geographical concepts to the phenomena under investigation, including space, place, scale, landscape, mobility, and nature. These concepts foreground the notion that the world operates spatially and temporally, and that social relations do not operate independently of place and environment, but are thoroughly grounded in and through them.

With respect to methods, human geography uses the full sweep of quantitative and qualitative methods from across the social sciences and humanities, mindful of using them to provide a thorough geographic analysis. It also places emphasis on fieldwork and mapping (see cartography), and has made a number of contributions to developing new methods and techniques, notably in the areas of spatial analysis, spatial statistics, and GI Science.

The long-term development of human geography has progressed in tandem with that of the discipline more generally (see geography). Since the Quantitative Revolution in the 1950s and 1960s, the philosophy underpinning human geography research has diversified enormously. The 1970s saw the introduction of behavioural geography radical geography, and humanistic geography. These were followed in the 1980s by a turn to political economy, the development of feminist geography, and the introduction of a critical social theory underpinning the cultural turn. Together these approaches formed the basis for the growth of critical geography, and the introduction of post modern and post-structural thinking into the discipline in the 1990s. These various developments did not fully replace the theoretical approaches developed in earlier periods, but rather led to further diversification of geographic thought. For example, quantitative geography continues to be a vibrant area of geographical scholarship, especially through the growth of GI Science. The result is that geographical thinking is presently highly pluralist in nature, with no one approach dominating.

1.1 Definitions and Meaning of Human Geography

1.1.1 Definitions

Following are some of the definitions given by scholars :

(i) According to **Ellsworth Huntington** , "*Human Geography is the study of the relationship of geographical environment to human activities and qualities.*"

(ii) According to **Jean Bruhnes**, "*Human Geography is a realm of compromise between human and natural form, study of human occupations and natural factors affecting them.*"

(iii) According to **Miss Ellen Semple**, "*Human Geography is a study of the changing relationships between the unresting man and unstable earth.*"

(iv) According to **White** and **Renner**, "*Study of relationships of natural factors and man with respect to man's compromise with natural environment*".

(v) According to **P. M. Roxby**, "*study of the adjustment of human groups to their physical environment and interrelationships of various groups of people within the region.*"

(vi) According to **D. H. Davis**, "*Human Geography is the search of natural cause-effect between geographical environment and human advancement.*"

(vii) According to **Lebon**, "*study of difference with respect to food, clothes, residence and occupations of man.*"

(viii) According to **Friedrich Ratzel**, Human Geography is the "*study of mutual relationships between man and environment.*"

(ix) According to **Cocks**, "*Human Geography is the description and interpretation of local patterns of stable and unstable facts created by man on earth*".

(x) According to **Vidal de la Blache,** "*Human Geography is the expression of growth of ideas rather than material result of discovery and extension of geographical knowledge.*"

1.1.2 Meaning

Geography deals with the distribution of various phenomena over the earth, which may include land, air, water, commodities such as wood, minerals and animal products. Everything which goes to make up man's environment forms part of the subject of human geography. Therefore, the study of human geography deals, mainly with the inter-relationship and interaction among man and his surrounding, both physical and biological (known as environment nowadays).

1.1.3 Importance

Importance of Human Geography :

(i) The value of studies in Human Geography is very great. In the first place, by understanding the cultural and social differences between human groups, and their relationship not only with the part of the earth in which they live but also with their economic activities, we can gain knowledge and sympathy with their problems which we could acquire in no other way.

(ii) An understanding of the geographical background will enable us to interpret their economic and political activities and attitudes, even though these may be entirely different from our own.

(iii) Another valuable aspect of human geography is that it shows how every part of the world is interdependent and cannot prosper in isolation.

(iv) Both physical factors and economic conditions are always interlinked with each other. For example, industrial countries depend for their imports of raw materials and for their export markets on the agricultural fields. On the other hand, agricultural fields depend on the industrial countries to absorb their surplus production.

(v) Where the Tropics depend on Temperate for their fruits and daily products, the Temperate zones depend on Tropical countries for crops, fruits and oilseeds.

(vi) Thus, a realisation of the interdependence of economies in different parts of the world will also promote a worldwide outlook rather than a narrow, local or regional one.

(vii) Finally, a knowledge of earth's resources and their exploitation by man can have great importance for the future generation.

(viii) The mishandling of soil, forests, fishes, minerals and so many other natural resources and the spoilation of natural environment may serve as lessons for the future, so that mistakes made in one part of the world need not be repeated in another.

1.2 Branches of Human Geography

Branches of Human Geography :

(i) In a narrow sense, the term 'Human Geography' has been defined as the "systematic study of the relationship between human societies and the environment."

(ii) In 1930's, the discipline of human geography was divided into 'Cultural geography' and 'Economic geography' and subsequently several new branches like Political geography, Social geography, Agricultural geography, Industrial geography, Settlement geography, Urban geography, Transport geography, Crime geography, Statistical geography, Medical geography and Geography of Gender emerged out of Human geography.

(iii) By the 1980's, human geography has widened to become an 'omnibus' term, describing all those parts of geography which are not solely concerned either with the physical environment or with the technical issues dealt with under such geographical sub-fields as cartography.

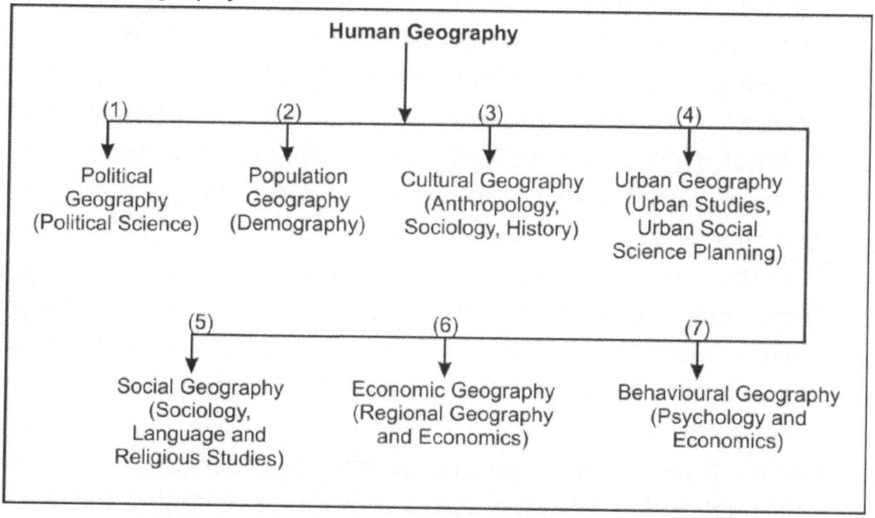

Fig. 1.1 Sub-divisions of Human Geography

(1) Political Geography

- **Political Geography (Meaning) :** Political geography is concerned with the study of both the spatially uneven results of political processes and the ways in which political processes are themselves affected by spatial structures. The primary concerns of the sub discipline can be summarized as the inter-relationships between people, state, and territory.
- From the late-1970s onwards, political geography has changed a lot and can be described as one of the most dynamic of the sub-disciplines today. The revival was due to the launch of the journal Political Geography Quarterly. Partly this growth has been associated with the adoption by political geographers up earlier in other areas of human geography.
- The recent growth in vitality and importance of this sub-discipline is related to the changes in the world due to end of the Cold War. With the emergence of a new world order (which as yet, is only poorly defined) and the development of new research agendas, such as the more recent focus on social movements and political struggles, going beyond the study of nationalism with its explicit territorial basis. There has also been increasing interest in the geography of green politics including the geopolitics of environmental protest, and in the capacity of our existing state apparatus and wider political institutions, to address any contemporary and future environmental problems competently.
- Political geography has increased the scope of traditional political science approaches by acknowledging that the exercise of power is not restricted to states and bureaucracies, but is part of everyday life.
- This has resulted in the concerns of political geography increasingly overlapping with human geography sub-disciplines such as economic geography, and, particularly, with those of social and cultural geography in relation to the study of the politics of place.

  Contemporary political geography often considers :
- The relationship between states and former colonies and neo-colonialism.

- How and why states are organized into regional groupings.
- The relationship between a government and its people.
- The relationships between states including trades and treaties.
- The functions, demarcations and policing of boundaries.
- How imagined geographies have political implications.
- The influence of political power on geographical space.
- The political implications of modern media.
- The study of election results.

(2) Population Geography :

- **Population Geography (Meaning) :** Population geography is a division of human geography. It is the study of the ways in which spatial variations in the distribution, composition, migration, and growth of populations are related to the nature of places. It gives importance to the characteristics of population distributions that change in a spatial context. It involves factors such as where population are found and how the size and composition of these population is regulated by the demographic processes such as fertility, mortality, and migration. Related disciplines include geography, demography, sociology, and economics.
- Since the beginning population geography has taken atleast three distinct but related forms, the most recent of which appears increasingly integrated with human geography in general. The earliest and most enduring form of population geography emerged in the 1950s, as part of spatial science.

Population geography defined itself as the systematic study of :

(a) The explanation of the spatial configuration of these numbers and characteristics.

(b) The simple description of the location of population numbers and characteristics.

(c) The geographic analysis of population phenomena.

- It categorized population as groups with political jurisdictions representing gender, religion, age, disability, generation, sexuality, and race, variables which go beyond the vital statistics of births, deaths, and marriages.

- Examples can be shown through population density maps i.e. choropleth, isoline, and dot maps.

Topics in Population Geography include the following :

- Demographic phenomena (such as nasality, mortality, growth rates, etc.) through space and time.
- Increases or decreases in population.
- The mobility of populations.
- Occupational structure.
- The way in which places in turn react to population phenomena, e.g. immigration.

(3) Cultural geography

- **Cultural Geography (Meaning) :** Cultural geography is a subfield within human geography. Cultural geography as academic study emerged as an alternative to the environmental determinist theories of the early twentieth century, which stated that people and societies are controlled by the environment in which they develop. Rather than studying pre-determined regions based upon environmental classifications, cultural geography became interested in cultural landscapes. It was done by Carl O. Sauer (called the father of cultural geography), at the University of California.
- This interaction between the natural landscape and humans creates the cultural landscape.

  This geography studies

  (i) Cultural a real differentiation, as a study of differences in way of life encompassing ideas, attitudes, languages, practices, institutions and structures of power and a whole range of cultural practices in geographical areas.

  (ii) Theories of cultural hegemony or cultural assimilation via cultural imperialism.

  (iii) Other topics are sense of place, colonialism, post-colonialism internationalism, immigration, emigration and ecotourism.

  (iv) Study of cultural landscapes and cultural ecology.

(4) Urban Geography :

- **Urban Geography (Meaning) :** Urban geography is the subdiscipline of geography that comes from a study of cities and urban processes. Various aspects of urban life and the built environment are studied. Scholars, activists, and the public have participated and, studied, the flows of economic and natural resources, human and non-human bodies, patterns of development and infrastructure, political and institutional activities, governance, decay and renewal, socio-spatial inclusions exclusions etc.
- Urban geographers are concerned with the ways in which cities and towns are constructed, governed etc. Alongwith disciplines such as urban anthropology, urban planning and urban sociology urban geography investigates the effect of urban processes on the earth's surface along with social and physical structures.
- Urban geographical research can be part of both human geography and physical geography.
- From the geographic perspective are the two fundamental aspects of cities and towns.

(a) Location spatial distribution and the complex patterns of movement, flows and linkages that bind them in space.

(b) Urban structure study of patterns of distribution and interaction within cities, from quantitative, qualitative, structural, and behavioural perspectives.

Research topics

(i) Cities as centers of manufacturing and services

- Cities differ in economy their social and demographic features and the roles they play within the city system. One can trace these differences back to regional variations in the local resources on which growth took place was during the early development of the urban pattern and in subsequent shifts in the competitive advantage of regions brought about by changing locational forces affecting regional specialization within the framework of a market economy.

- The simplest way to classify cities is to identify the unique and different role they play in the city system.

  The three distinct roles are as follows :

  - central places functioning primarily as service centers for local hinterlands.
  - transportation cities performing break-of-bulk and allied functions for larger regions.
  - specialized-function cities, dominated by one activity such as mining, manufacturing or recreation and serving national and international markets.

(ii) Urbanization :

- Urbanization, the transformation of population from rural to urban, is a major phenomenon of the modern era and a central topic of study

(5) Social Geography :

- **Social Geography (Meaning) :** Social geography is the branch of human geography that is closely related to social theory in general and sociology in particular, dealing with the relation of social phenomena and its spatial components.
- According to Anne Buttimer "social geography can be considered a field created and cultivated by a number of individual scholars rather than an academic tradition built up within particular schools".
- The different conceptions of social geography overlap with other sub-fields of geography and, to a lesser extent, sociology.

  When the term emerged it was basically applied as a synonym for the search for patterns in the distribution of social groups, thus being closely connected to urban geography and urban sociology.
- Within some continental European traditions, social geography is considered an approach to human geography rather than a sub-discipline, or even as identical to human geography in general.
- The term "social geography" (or rather "*géographie sociale*") originates from France, where it was used both by geographer Élisée Reclus and by sociologists of the Le Play School.

- The first person in the Anglo-American tradition to use the term "social geography" was **George Wilson Hoke,** whose paper The Study of Social Geography was published in 1907.

(6) Economic Geography :

Economic Geography (Meaning) : Economic geography is the subfield of geography which studies the influence of geography on economic activity. It is also considered a subfield in economics.

- Economic geography adopts many approaches to many topics, including the location of industries, economies of agglomeration, transportation, international trade, development, real estate, gentrification, ethnic economies, gendered economies, core-periphery theory, the economics of urban form, the relationship between the environment and the economy and globalization.
- There are different methodological approaches. Neoclassical location theorists, following in the tradition of Alfred Weber, tend to focus on industrial location and use quantitative methods.
- Economists such as Paul Krugman and Jeffrey Sachs have also analyzed many traits related to economic geography.
- Early approaches to economic geography are found in the seven Chinese maps of the State of Qin, and in the Greek geographer Strabo's Geographika, almost 2000 years ago.
- World War II contributed to the popularization of geographical knowledge and post-war economic recovery and development contributed to the growth of economic geography as a discipline.
- At present economic geographers tend to specialize in areas such as location theory and spatial analysis market research, geography of transportation, real estate price evaluation, regional and global development, planning, Internet geography, innovation, social networks.

Approaches to study

- Economic geographers have adopted some distinct approaches to study and have evolved over time.

(a) Regional economic geography studies the economic conditions of particular regions or countries of the world. It deals with economic regionalization as well as local economic development.

(b) Theoretical economic geography emphasizes building theories about spatial arrangement and distribution of economic activities.

(c) Historical economic geography studies the history and development of spatial economic structure. Using historical data, it examines how centers of population and economic activity shift, what patterns of regional specialization and localization evolve over time and what factors explain these changes.

(d) Evolutionary economic geography adopts an evolutionary approach to economic geography. More specifically, Evolutionary economic geography uses concepts and ideas from evolutionary economics to understand the evolution of cities, regions, and other economic systems.

(e) Critical economic geography is an approach taken from the point of view of contemporary critical geography and its philosophy.

(f) Behavioral economic geography examines the cognitive processes underlying spatial reasoning, locational decision making, and behaviour of firms and individuals.

- Economic geography is sometimes seen as a branch of anthropogeography that emphasizes regional systems of human economic activity.

Branches

- Economic geography can be divided into the following subdisciplines :

(i) Geography of agriculture

(ii) Geography of industry

(iii) Geography of international trade

(iv) Geography of resources

(v) Geography of transport and communication

(vi) Geography of finance

(7) Behavioural Geography (Meaning) :

- Behavioural geography is an approach to human geography that examines human behaviour using a disaggregate approach. Behavioural geographers focus on the cognitive processes underlying spatial reasoning, decision making, and behavior.
- Behavioral geography is that branch of human science, which deals with the study of cognitive processes with its response to environment, through behaviourism.
- Because of the name it is often assumed to have its roots in behaviorism. While some behavioral geographers clearly have roots in behaviourism due to the emphasis on cognition, most can be seen as cognitively oriented.
- Behavioural geography is influenced by early behaviorist works such as Tolman's concepts of "cognitive maps".
- The approach adopted in behavioural geography is closely related to that of psychology, but draws on research findings from disciplines such as economics, sociology, anthropology, transportation, planning etc.

1.3 Nature and Scope of Human Geography

1.3.1 Nature of Human Geography

Nature of Human Geography :

(i) Man is a geographical agent, also an active creature who makes adjustment with his physical environment and changes the shape of natural resources and makes the greatest use of them. In this way, man influences his environment or surroundings.

(ii) The mutual synthesis between man and natural environment is studied in human geography.

(iii) In other words, human geography is that part of the discipline of geography, which deals with the spatial differentiation and organisation of human activity and with human use of the physical environment. It can be said that human geography studies the adjustment with surroundings on the regional basis and we study its mutual relationship.

Human Ecology and Human Geography :

(i) The American geographers who were the believers of social Darwinism first introduced the concept of human ecology.

(ii) It was H. H. Barrow, who in his presidential address to the Association of American Geographers in 1923, declared that "human geography is human ecology". The followers of this school tried to establish an interactive relation between man and his biotic and abiotic elements of environment.

(iii) The central idea of human ecology is that man like plants and animals has to struggle in his physical environment and in the process of struggle, the weaker get eliminated.

(iv) The discipline of human geography as human ecology was further strengthened by the works of Lamarekian, who emphasized that organisms could consciously adapt themselves to their surroundings and pass on acquired characteristics to offsprings.

(v) The approach of taking human geography as human ecology has however been criticised on several grounds. The critics said that man is a tool making, tool using and culture making animal who can transform the habitats and ecosystems drastically through his knowledge of innovation and scientific advancement.

The Relationship between Man and his Environment :

(i) According to one of the popular and widely accepted definitions, human geography is the study of "man and his adjustment to his natural environment".

(ii) According to **Jean Brunches,** who was a follower of Blache, human geography is the relationship between unresting and the unstable earth which is called civilisation and culture in the form of human responses.

(iii) The development of the civilisation depends on closer interactions between a land and its people.

(iv) A popular school of geographical thought in the early 1900's was that of 'Environmental Determinism' or 'Environmentalism', which mentioned that the physical environment determined man's economic activities.

(v) White and Renner also established the mutual relationship between human society and earth background and they called it human geography. Sample, another geographer also described "human geography is a study of the changing relationship between the unresting man and the unstable earth.

(vi) According to another branch of geographers, there are numerous racial and ethnic groups in the world and the geo-climatic conditions of the various parts of the earth also differ from each other substantially.

(vii) Each society or ethnic group uses the natural resources according to its cultural stage and technological advancement. For example, the mode of life of Pygmies of Congo basin differs from that of the Bedouins of Saudi Arabia.

(ix) These variations in the lifestyle, are expressions of man's adjustment to his natural environment.

(x) Food, clothing, shelter, tools, technology, customs, traditions, socio-economic institutions, higher needs like religion, faith, language, literature, fine arts and folklore etc. are all aspects of life directly or indirectly influenced by the physical environment.

(xi) In other words, man has moulded his habitats and lifestyle according to his physical surroundings and natural endowments. For example, the mobile hunting and fishing have allowed the Eskimos to survive in the inhospitable Arctic (– 50°C) temperature with their primitive technology. The nomadic pastoralism in Saudi Arabia and Sahara deserts provides a livelihood to the Bedouins and Tuareg. Other example of man's adjustment to his environment may be cited from the mountainous areas of the world. The hilly and mountainous areas always give rise to closed societies, self centered, orthodox and preserving old customs.

(xii) The indigenous people have adjusted well in their natural environment without disturbing the ecological balance, though their economies are often called primitive, their technology dismissed as 'Stone Age'.

(xiii) From the above points of view, we can say that man adapts his life either wholly or in part in particular ways with physical and organic nature in order to pass his life with physical environment.

1.3.2 Scope of Human Geography

The subject matter of human geography may be divided into two broad sections viz. : (i) Physical or natural environment and

(ii) Cultural or man-made environment.

According to Finch and Trewartha, the presentation of human facts on a regional basis and the systematic study and distribution of human facts on the surface of the earth is the subject matter of cultural or human geography.

(i) It also studies the human societies and their relation to the habitat or environment. Thus, it covers a very wide field or its scope is enormous.

(ii) Human geography studies human races, the growth, distribution and density of population of the various parts of the world, their demographic attributes and migration patterns and physical and cultural differences between human groups and economic activities.

(iii) Human culture, language, religion, customs, traditions, various forms of rural settlement, types and growth of urban settlements, functional classification of towns etc. are all the subject matter of human geography.

(iv) The study of spatial distribution of economic activities, industries, trade and mode of transportation and communication as influenced by the physical environment are also the important topics of human geography.

(v) In brief in human geography, we study influence of physical environment on the economic activity, society, culture and religion of the people of a region.

(vi) The adjustment of man to his physical environment in typical geographical regions like equatorial, hot deserts and Tundra is of great relevance to human geography as it helps in understanding the symbiotic relationship between social groups and their natural environment.

(vii) Human geography also deals with the livelihood patterns of people of various countries. Its emphasizes on how people interact over space and time and what kinds of landscapes of human use they erect upon the natural landscapes they occupy.

(viii) Human geography's content provides integration for all the social sciences, for it gives to those sciences the necessary spatial, temporal and system's view point that they otherwise lack.

(ix) At the same time, human geography draws on other social sciences in the analyses identified with its sub-fields such as behavioural, political, economic or social geography.

(x) Human geography admirably serves the objectives of a liberal education. It helps us to understand the world we occupy and to appreciate the circumstances affecting people and nations other than our own.

(xi) It clarifies the contrasts in societies and cultures and in the human landscapes they have created in different regions of the earth.

(xii) Its models and explanations of spatial interaction allow us to better comprehend the economic, social and political systems within which we all, singly and collectively live and operate.

1.4 Contemporary Relevance of Human Geography

- The major concepts of human geography i.e. – location, distribution, space, place, region, movement, diffusion and man-environment interrelationships have contemporary relevance.
- Contemporary human geography does a scientific study of location of people and activities on the earth surface and the causes for their distribution including density, concentration and pattern analysis. In human geography population studies include population growth trends and patterns, density and distribution in context of physical and cultural landscape.
- Determinants of population dynamics – fertility, mortality and migration are key concerns.
- Population-resource-development relationships and population problems provide insights for population policy formulations.

- The study of population is the basis for understanding many different issues in human geography.
- To understand the challenges of increasing food supply, reducing poverty and inequalities, encouraging economic growth with distributive justice and ecological balance and reducing pollution the modern human geographers focus on quantitative as well as qualitative aspects.
- The insider-outsider conflicts due to migration and refugee problems have gained significance in contemporary human geography. Human geographers try to understand and explain why differences exist and how social customs are related to cultural landscape.
- It assists in understanding cultural features such as religions languages and ethnicities on the earth. Human geography explains the contrasts in societies and cultures and in the human landscapes they have created in different parts of the world. In contemporary times people are being pulled in opposite directions by two factors – globalization and local diversity. Political conflicts, economic uncertainty and pollution are reflections of these two opposite forces. Within human geography political geographers help to explain the physical and cultural elements that form the basis of political unrest in the world. Human geographers are different from other social scientists because they never forget physical environment as they are trained in both social and physical-biological sciences.
- This is significant very in studies related to natural disasters and their management and mitigation. This integrated approach has also special significance in achieving the goal of substation development.
- Human geographers address urban problems and help in process of sustainable urbanization. The concepts, explanations, models and theories of human geography help in clear understanding to interconnections of the physical, economic, social and political systems within which we live and operate.

- The analysis of these interconnections makes us aware about the realities and prospects of our own society in a competitive world. This way human geography helps in developing more informed citizens, more capable of understanding present day challenges faced by communities and countries and finally better prepared to contribute in overcoming these challenges.
- Human geography as a second major branch of geography focuses on the study of people and their social groups, cultures, economies, and interactions with the environment by studying their relations in spatiotemporal perspective.
- Human geography is the study of the changing relationship between the active man and dynamic earth surface features. The major branches of human geography are population geography, settlement geography, economic geography, socio-cultural geography, political geography, medical geography, behavioural and environmental geography.
- Human geography helps in developing better informed citizens and better human beings, more capable of understanding contemporary challenges faced by communities and countries and finally better prepared for mitigating these challenges.

POINTS TO REMEMBER

- Human Geography is the study of the interrelationships between people, place and environment and how these vary spatially and temporally across and between locations.
- The value of studies in Human Geography is very great.
- In 1930's the discipline of human geography was divided into 'Cultural Geography' and 'Economic geography' and subsequently several new branches were adopted.
- The subject matter of human geography may be divided into two broad sections viz. (i) Physical or natural environment and (ii) Cultural or man-made environment.

✧ QUESTIONS ✧

Q. I : Answer the following questions in detail.

(1) *Define Human Geography. Give it's meaning.*

(2) *Write in detail about the branches of Human Geography.*

(3) *State the nature of Human Geography.*

(4) *What is the scope of Human Geography ?*

(5) *Write about the contemporary relevance of Human Geography.*

Q. II : Write short notes :

(1) *Political Geography*

(2) *Population Geography*

(3) *Urban Geography*

(4) *Human Geography*

(5) *Human ecology and Human Geography*

❋ ❋ ❋

UNIT – 2

HUMAN EVOLUTION AND RACES

SYNOPSIS

INTRODUCTION

The Human evolution process has led to the emergence of present anatomically modern humans, beginning with primates in particular genus Homo and leading to the emergence of Homo sapiens as a unique species of the hominid family. It involved the gradual development of traits such as human bipedalism and language, as well as interbreeding with other hominins.

Human evolution includes many scientific disciplines, i. e. physical anthropology, primatology, archaeology, paleontology, neurobiology ethology, linguistics, evolutionary, psychology, embryology and genetics.

Human evolution from its separation from the last common ancestor of humans and chimpanzees has undergone morphological, developmental, physiological and behavioral changes the most significant adaptations are bipedalism, increased brain size, lengthened ontogeny and decreased sexual dimorphism.

- Bipedalism is the basic adaptation of the hominids and is considered the main reason behind many skeletal changes shared by all bipedal hominids. The non-bipedal gorillas and chimpanzees, separated from the hominin line over a period covering the same time.
- Anatomically, the evolution of bipedalism has taken place in a large number of skeletal changes, not just to the legs and pelvis, but also to the vertebral column, feet and ankles, and skull.
- The human species eventually developed a much larger brain than that of other primates.
- Many other changes have characterized the evolution of humans, i. e. increased importance on sight rather than smell; a longer juvenile developmental period and higher infant dependency smaller gut; faster basal metabolism loss of body hair; evolution of sweat glands; a change in the shape of the dental arcade, development of a chin etc.

2.1 Stages of Human Evolution

There is no such established evidence to prove when the first man appeared on the earth and at which place he was born. About the evolution of early man, we may however learn something in two different ways (i) by comparing the biology of man with that of other animals and so determining the degree of their relationship and (ii) by looking at fossils and so determining their age and development.

(a) Primates : Man is a primate or one of the highest group of mammals. He had a large brain, a grasping hand with big nails and large eyesight which has been developed at the expense of his sense of smell.

- Within the group of shrews, lemurs, monkeys and apes, man shows the greatest resemblance to apes. Man has been distinguished from other primates, both living and fossils, by his ability to make and use tools.
- During the period of the Tertiary Era, man lived both upon the ground and in trees like apes. They could rapidly move through a forest without descending to the ground and so they are secured from capture by more powerful carnivorous land animals.

(b) **Adaptation** : At the first time, humans were essentially quadrupeds and had prehensile tail. In the later stage, man had no use of a tail. His feet have became fully adapted for walking and running. As there is no requirement for walking or for grasping branches during leaps from tree to tree, the hand has become a precisely controlled organ.

- Adaptation of an erect posture has been accompanied by enlargement of the brain, especially of the front, which is the seat of the higher intellectual function. The eye has become elaborated and human vision is fully stereoscopic, unlike that of any other animal.
- A dimination of the jaw and its controlling muscles appear to have accompanied the increasing variety of food, with greater intelligence he could command and, in the later stages of evolution, prepare for convenient eating.

(c) **Work Specialisation** : Then the differentiation of work and specialisation between males and females developed. The former obtain food and protect the family, the latter hand the young ones and prepare food.

- Thus, the family finds its origin in the mutual dependence of male, female and the young.

(d) **Hunting :** When primitive man became a hunter, the change of food habits are also found. They added animals as food with fruits, nuts and edible shoots.

- At the same time hair growth was arrested, for modern man apart from the head and certain other localized parts of the body, grows only sparse, very fine hair.

(e) **Pleistocene period :** During the age of the Pleistocene period, final stage of human evolution took place. At that time, the world's climate approached great oscillations. During the Tertiary Era the land areas of the world, particularly in the middle and higher latitudes of the northern hemisphere, were less extensive then today, and the climate generally milder.

- Forests of a tropical or sub-tropical character were more widespread, and it may be inferred that the precursors of both modern apes and men were widely dispersed. But, in the Pleistocene period, great uplifts of land, constituting the final phase of recent world wide mountain building, increased both the extent of land and its attitude.

- Large areas became remote from the sea and some were shielded from rain bearing winds by the higher mountains. It was in such a world that man's ape like forebears became wholly terrestrial and more carnivorous.
- Reduction of hair growth in human beings would be unthinkable in a more severe climate, which would tend to encourage a shaggier growth; and until perhaps the most recent stage in human evolution. During the latest phases of Pleistocene, when culture had become fairly elaborate, Prehominids or men like apes were confined to warm climates.
- So, the fragments of primitive skulls and skeletons were discovered in parts of Tropics and sub-tropical latitudes of Asia, Africa and Europe. Thus, men became adapted to a fairly range of warmer climates and towards the polar margins of his habitat must have become accustomed to seasonal change of temperature.

(f) Inter-glacial periods : During the inter-glacial periods, much of Europe, Northern and Central Asia were covered by permanent ice-sheets. On the other hand, the Arctic and Sub-arctic climatic zones prevailed as far South latitudes 40° in the northern hemisphere.

- So the primitive stone tools have been discovered in Europe and Northern China, worn by the action of ice and running water. During the first three glacial-periods, the ancestors of humanity were compelled to retreat towards the tropics.
- Thus, each glaciation was a crisis not only for evolving Prehominids, but for all focus of the life and many species of plants and animals which flourished at the end of the Tertiary Era failed to survive on Itolocene.
- Ape-men, moving to and fro across the world, were confronted with new perils and new economic crisis, which their greater mental powers overcame.
- By the third inter-glacial period, between the Riss and Warm glaciations, men were able to make tools and weapons from stone and also from wood and bone of animals. During the

fourth glacial period, they were able to survive in more rigorous climates not by retreat into warmer regions, but to caves, where by the use of fire and skin garments, they could continue to live close to the glaciers and ice-sheets.

- Among the best known of these early races was Neanderthalman, having larger bones and more powerful muscles than modern man, and possessing a more primitive skull with protruding, massive jaw, a receding forehead and a very prominent bony ridge above the eyes. Neanderthaloids appear to have evolved as a separate race north of the Tertiary Mountain Belt of Europe and Asia.

(g) Modern Humans : The term anatomically modern human (AMH) or atomically modern 'Homo sapiens (AMHS) refer to Paleoanthropology to individual members of the species Homo Sapiens.

Human Evolution (Meaning) :

- Human evolution is that part of biological evolution concerning the emergence of humans as a distinct species. It seeks to understand and describe how this change and development occurred. The study of human evolution encompasses most notably physical anthropology, linguistics and genetics.

History of Paleoanthropology :

- Modern paleoanthropology began in the 19th century with the discovery of "Neanderthal man" and with evidence of so-called cave men. The idea of the biological evolution of species in general was not legitimized till after Charles Darwin published a books called *'On the Origin of Species'* in 1859.
- Huxley illustrated many of the similarities and differences between humans and apes in his 1863 book.
- In the 19th century, it was thought that the closest living relatives were chimpanzees and gorillas, and it was surmised that humans share a common ancestor with African apes and that fossils would be ultimately found in Africa.
- It was not till the 1920s that hominin fossils were discovered in Africa. In 1924, Raymond Dart described Australopithecus africanus. Traits convinced Dart that the Taung baby was a bipedal human ancestor, a transitional form between apes and humans.

- The australopithecines are now taken as immediate ancestors of the genus Homo, the group to which modern humans belong. Both australopithecines and Homo sapiens are part of the tribe Hominini, but recent data has brought into doubt the position of A. africanus as a direct ancestor of modern humans. The robust variety of Australopithecus has since been reclassified as Paranthropus. During the 1960s, the robust variety was moved into Australopithecus.

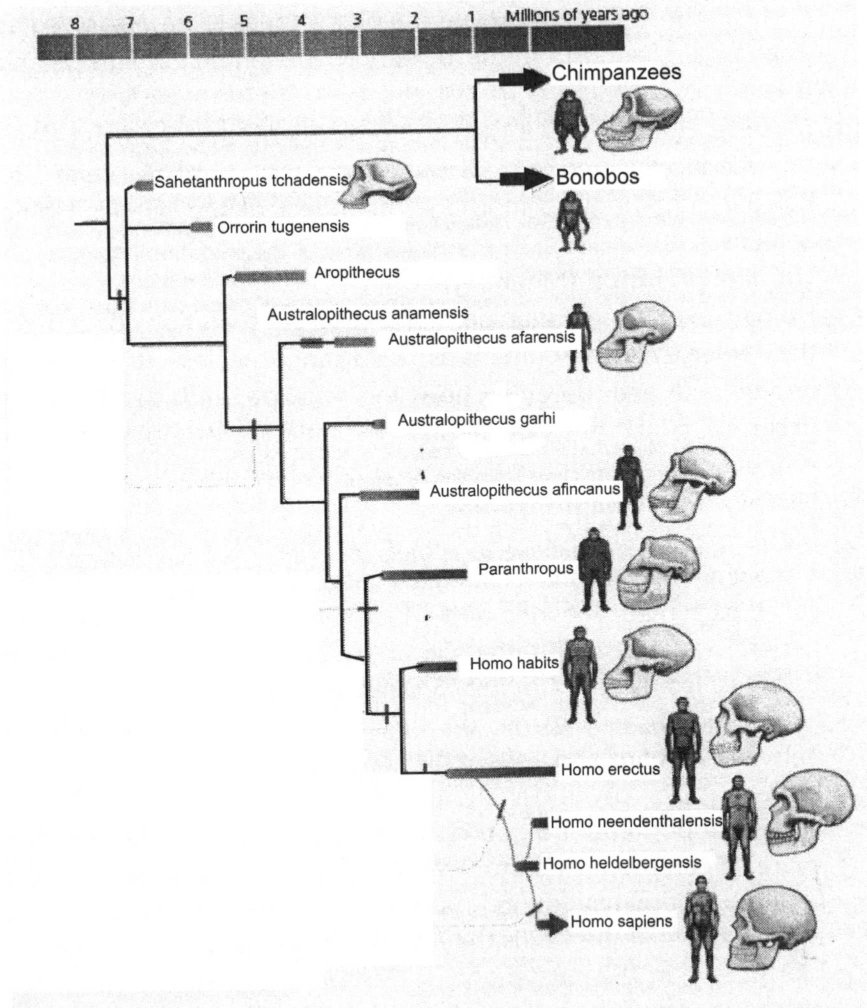

Fig. 2.1 : Evolution of Human Species

- The discoveries suggest that the early ancestors of the hominids (the family of great apes and humans) migrated to Eurasia from Africa about 17 million years ago. Begun says that the great apes flourished in Eurasia and that their lineage leading to the African apes and humans - Dryopithecus - migrated south from Europe or Western Asia into Africa.
- The earliest known catarrhine is Kamoyapithecus from uppermost Oligocene at Eragaleit in the northern Kenya rift valley, dated to 24 Ma (millions of years before present). Its ancestry is generally thought to be close to such general as Aegyptopithecus and Parapithecus from the Fayum, at around 35 Ma.
- Among the presently recognized genera in this group, which ranges up to 13 Ma, we find Proconsul, Rangwapithecus, Dendropithecus, Limnopithecus, Nacholapithecus, Equatorius, Ny anzapithecus, Afropithecus, Heliopithecus, and Kenyapithecus, all from East Africa.
- The presence of other generalized non cercopithecids of middle Miocene age from sites far distant Otavipithecus from cave deposits in Namibia and Pieroloapithecus and Dryopithecus from France, Spain and Austria. The youngest of the Miocene hominoids, Oreopithecus, is from 9-Ma coal beds in Italy.
- Fossil proto-orangutans may be represented by Ramapithecus from India and Griphopithecus from Turkey, dated to around 10 Ma.
- Evidence further suggests that between 8 and 4 MYA, first the gorillas, and then the chimpanzee (genus Pan) split off from the line leading to the humans.
- Homo sapiens is the only extant species of its genus, Homo.
- The word homo is Latin for "person", chosen originally by Carolus Linnaeus in his classification system.

Homo habilis :

- H. habilis lived from about 2.4 to 1.5 million years ago (MYA). H. habilis, the first species of the genus Homo, evolved in South and

East Africa in the late Pliocene or early Pleistocene, 2.5–2 MYA, when it diverged from the Australopithecines.

Homo rudolfensis and Homo georgicus

These are proposed species names for fossils from about 1.9-1.6 MYA, the relation of which with H. habilis is not yet clear.

- H. rudolfensis refers to a single, incomplete skull from Kenya.
- H. georgicus, from Georgia, may be an intermediate form between H. habilis and H. erectus.

Homo ergaster and Homo erectus

- The first fossils of homo erectus were discovered by Dutch physician Eugene Dubois in 1891 on the Indonesian island of Java. He originally gave the material the name Pithecanthropus erectus based on its morphology apes.
- In the Early Pleistocene, 1.5–1 MYA, in Africa, Asia, and Europe, presumably, Homo habilis evolved larger brains and made more elaborate stone tools; these differences and others are sufficient for anthropologists to classify them as a new species, H. erectus.

Homo cepranensis and Homo antecessor

These are proposed as species that may be intermediate between H. erectus and H. heidelbergensis.

- H. cepranensis refers to a single skull cap from Italy, estimated to be about 800,000 years old.
- H. antecessor is known from fossils from Spain and England that are 800,000-500,000 years old.

Homo heidelbergensis

- H. heidelbergensis (Heidelberg Man) lived from about 800,000 to about 300,000 years ago. Also proposed as Homo sapiens heidelbergensis or Homo sapiens paleohungaricus.

Homo neanderthalensis

- H. neanderthalensis lived from about 350,000 to as recent as 30,000 years ago. Also proposed as Homo sapiens neanderthalensis.

Homo rhodesiensis and the Gawis cranium

- H. rhodesiensis, estimated to be 300,000-125,000 years old, most current experts believe Rhodesian Man to be within the group of Homo heidelbergensis though other designations such as Archaic Homo sapiens and Homo sapiens rhodesiensis have also been proposed.
- In February 2006 a fossil, the Gawis cranium, was found which might possibly be a species intermediate between H. erectus and H. sapiens or one of many evolutionary dead ends.

Homo sapiens

- H. sapiens has lived from about 200,000 years ago to the present. Between 400,000 years ago and the second interglacial period in the Middle Pleistocene, around 250,000 years ago, the trend in cranial expansion and the elaboration of stone tool technologies developed, providing evidence for a transition from H. erectus to H. sapiens.
- Current research establishes that human beings are highly genetically homogenous, meaning that the DNA of individual Homo sapiens is more alike than usual for most species, a result of their relatively recent evolution.
- H. sapiens idaltu, from Ethiopia, lived from about 160,000 years ago (proposed subspecies). It is the oldest known anatomically modern human.

Homo floresiensis

- H. floresiensis, which lived about 100,000 - 12,000 years ago (announced 28 October 2004 in the science journal Nature), has been nicknamed hobbit for its small size, probably a result of insular (island) dwarfism. H. floresiensis is intriguing both for its size and its age, being a concrete example of a recent species of the genus Homo that exhibits derived traits not shared with modern humans. In other words.

Comparative table of Homo species

Bolded species names indicate the existence of numerous fossil records.

Table 2.1 : Comparative table of Homo Species

Species	Lived when (MYA)	Lived where	Adult length (m)	Adult weight (kg)	Brain volume (cm^3)	Fossil record	Discovery / Publication of name
H. habilis	2.5–1.5	Africa	1.0–1.5	30–55	600	many	1960 / 1964
H. rudolfensis	1.9	Kenya				1 skull	1972 / 1986
H. georgicus	1.8–1.6	Georgia			600	few	1999 / 2002
H. ergaster	1.9–1.25	E. and S. Africa	1.9		700–850	many	1975
H. erectus	2(1.25)–0.3	Africa, Eurasia (Java, China, Caucasus)	1.8	60	900–1100	many	1891 / 1892
H. cepranensis	0.8?	Italy				1 skull cap	1994 / 2003
H. antecessor	0.8–0.35	Spain, England	1.75	90	1000	3 sites	1997
H. heidelbergensis	0.6–0.25	Europe, Africa, China	1.8	60	1100–1400	many	1908
H.neanderthalensis	0.23–0.03	Europe, W. Asia	1.6	55–70 (heavily built)	1200-1700	many	1829 / 1864
H. rhodesiensis	0.3–0.12	Zambia			1300	very few	1921
H. sapiens	0.25–present	Worldwide	1.4–1.9	55–80	1000–1850	still living	1758
H. sapiens idaltu	0.16	Ethiopia			1450	3 craniums	1997 / 2003
H. floresiensis	0.10–0.012	Indonesia	1.0	25	400	7 individuals	2003 / 2004

Use of tools

- Early hominoids, like apes, were essentially plant eaters (fruit, leaves, roots), their diet only occasionally supplemented by meat (often from scavenging). However, plant food in general yields considerably less energy and nutritive value than meat. Therefore, being able to hunt for large animals, which was only possible by using tools such as spears, made it possible for humans to sustain larger and more complex brains, which in turn allowed them to develop yet more intelligent and efficient tools.

Stone tools

- Stone tools are first attested around 2.6 million years ago, when H. habilis in Eastern Africa used so-called pebble tools, choppers made out of round pebbles that had been split by simple strikes. This marks the beginning of the Paleolithic, or Old Stone Age; its end is taken to be the end of the last Ice Age, around 10,000 years ago.
- Finally, after about 50,000 BP, even more refined and specialized flint tools were made by the Neanderthals and the immigrant Cro-Magnons (knives, blades, skimmers). In this period they also started to make tools out of bone.

The "modern man" debate and the Great Leap Forward

- After 50,000 BP, what Jared Diamond, author of The Third Chimpanzee, and other anthropologists characterize as a Great Leap Forward, human culture apparently started to change at much greater speed: "modern" humans started to bury their dead carefully, made clothing out of hides, developed sophisticated hunting techniques and made cave paintings.
- This cultural change seems connected with the arrival of modern humans, homo sapiens. Additionally, human culture began to become more advanced, in that, different populations of humans begin to create novelty in existing technologies.

Species List

(i) Sahelanthropus

- Sahelanthropus tchadensis

(ii) Orrorin

- Orrorin tugenensis

(iii) Ardipithecus

- Ardipithecus kadabba

- Ardipithecus ramidus

(iv) Australopithecus

- Australopithecus anamensis
- Australopithecus afarensis
- Australopithecus bahrelghazali
- Australopithecus africanus
- Australopithecus garhi

(v) Paranthropus

- Paranthropus aethiopicus
- Paranthropus boisei
- Paranthropus robustus

(vi) Kenyanthropus

- Kenyanthropus platyops

(vii) Homo

- Homo habilis
- Homo rudolfensis
- Homo ergaster
- Homo georgicus
- Homo erectus
- Homo cepranensis
- Homo antecessor
- Homo heidelbergensis
- Homo rhodesiensis
- Homo neanderthalensis
- Homo sapiens idaltu
- Homo sapiens (Cro-magnon)
- Homo sapiens sapiens
- Homo floresiensis

2.2 Meaning and Definitions of Human Race

"A race is a biological inbreed group possessing a distinctive combination of physical traits that tend to breed true from generation to generation."

According to **A. L. Kroeber**, *"Race is a human group united by heredity, a breed or sub-species".*

Wellice defined, *"Race is a human group with homogeneous hereditary characters or biological traits".*

The races of the world are classified into five principal classes by some anthropologists and they are as follows : (i) The Negroid, (ii) Caucasoids - they are further categorized into : (a) Nordic, (b) Mediterranean, (c) Alpine, (iii) Mongoloid - they are categorised into : (a) Mongolian, (b) Eastern Archipelago, (c) North and South Americans, (iv) The Australoids, (v) Capoid.

- A race is a grouping of humans based on shared physical or social qualities into categories generally viewed as distinct by society. Modern scholarship regards race as a social construct, an identity which is assigned based on rules made by society.

Race : It is a valid biological concept : it denotes breed, not culture.

According to **Kroeber** "*A race is a valid biological concept, a breed or genetic strain or sub-species. It is not a valid socio-cultural concept.*"

According to J. B. Birdsell, "*A race is an interbreeding group whose gene pool is different from other populations.*"

According to Blache "*We understand race to mean classification based on somatic characteristics affecting the morphology or physiology of the human body.*"

Haddon considers race as a biological breed based on a combination of physical traits which are transmitted.

- Social conceptions of races differ over time, period involving folk taxonomies that define essential types of individuals based on traits.
- Scientists continue to conceptualize race in many differing ways, some of which have essentialist implications. Some researchers use the concept of race to make distinctions among confusing sets of traits or observable differences in behaviour. Others suggest that the idea of race often is used in a naive or simplistic way, and argue that, all living humans belong to the same species, Homo sapiens, and subspecies,
- Although still used in general contexts, race has often been replaced by less ambiguous and loaded terms, populations, people (s) ethnic groups, or communities etc.

Defining race

- Different cultures define different racial groups, often focused on the largest groups of social relevance, and these definitions can change over time.
- In South Africa, the Population Registration Act, 1950 recognized only White, Black, and Coloured and the government of Myanmar recognizes eight "major national ethnic races".
- The Brazilians classify people into brancos (whites), pardos (multiracial), pretos (blacks), caboclos, amarelos (Asians), and indigenous.
- Historical race concepts have included many schemes to divide local or worldwide populations into races and sub-races.
- The establishment of racial boundaries often involves the domination of groups defined as racially inferior. Such racial identities show the cultural attitudes of imperial powers dominant during the European colonial expansion. This view rejects the notion that race is biologically defined.
- According to geneticist David Reich, "while race may be a social construct, differences in genetic ancestry that happen to correlate to many of today's racial constructs are real."
- Although common physical traits such as facial features, skin colour, and hair comprise part of the race concept, this linkage is a social distinction rather than an inherently biological one. Other dimensions of racial groupings include shared history, traditions and language.
- When people define and talk about a particular conception of race, they create a social reality through which social categorization is achieved. In this sense, races are said to be social constructs.
- Socioeconomic factors, along with early but enduring views of race, have led to considerable suffering within disadvantaged racial groups.
- In some countries, law enforcement uses race to profile suspects. In 2008, John Hartigan, Jr. argued for a view of race that focused primarily on culture, but which does not ignore the potential relevance of biology or genetics.

- In the social sciences, theoretical frameworks such as racial formation theory and critical race theory investigate implications of race as social construction by exploring how the images, ideas and assumptions of race are expressed in everyday life.

Historical origins of racial classification

- The three great races according to Meyers Konversations-Lexikon of 1885-90. (i) The subtypes of the Mongoloid race are shown in yellow and orange tones, (ii) Caucasoid race in light and medium grayish spring green-cyan tones and (iii) Negroid race in brown tones. (iv) Dravidians and Sinhalese are in olive green. (v) The Mongoloid race sees the widest geographic distribution, including all of the Americas, North Asia, East Asia, and Southeast Asia, the entire inhabited Arctic while they form most of Central Asia and the Pacific Islands.
- Idea of race as we understand it today came about during the historical process of exploration and conquest which brought Europeans into contact with groups from different continents, and of the ideology of classification and typology found in the natural sciences.
- The term race was often used in a general biological taxonomic sense, starting from the 19th century, to denote genetically differentiated human populations defined by phenotype.
- The modern concept of race emerged due to colonial enterprises of European powers from the 16th to 18th centuries which identified race in terms of skin colour and physical differences.

Colonialism

- As Europeans came across people from different parts of the world, they speculated about the physical, social, and cultural differences among various human groups.
- Europeans began to categorize themselves and others into groups based on physical appearance, and to attribute to individuals belonging to these group behaviors and capacities which were claimed to be deeply ingrained.
- Similar ideas can be found in other cultures, for example in China, where a concept often translated as "race" was associated with

supposed common descent from the Yellow Emperor, and used to stress the unity of ethnic groups in China.

- In the 18th century the differences among human groups became a focus of scientific investigation. But the scientific classification of phenotypic variation was frequently coupled with racist ideas always attributing the most desirable features to the White, European race and arranging the other races along a progressively undesirable attributes. The 1735 classification of Carl Linnaeus, divided the human species Homo sapiens into continental varieties of europaeus, asiaticus, americanus, and after each associated with a different humour; sanguine, melancholic, choleric, and phlegmatic, respectively.
- In a 1775 treatise "The Natural Varieties of Mankind", by Johann Friedrich Blumenbach, he proposed five major divisions: the Caucasoid race, the Mongoloid race, the Ethiopian race (later termed Negroid), the American Indian race, and the Malayan race, but he did not propose any hierarchy among the races.
- According to "ideology of race" races are primordial, natural, enduring and distinct.
- It was further argued that some groups may be the result of mixture between formerly distinct populations, but that careful study could distinguish the ancestral races that had combined to produce admixed groups.
- In later 18th century, the theory of polygenism, the belief that different races had evolved separately in each continent and shared no common ancestor, was forwarded. Polygenism was popular and most widespread in the 19th century, culminating in the founding of the Anthropological Society of London (1863).

2.2.1 Classification of Races

(I) Classification : The races of the world are classified into five principle classes by some anthropologists and they are as follows :

(1) The Negroid :

(i) The Negroes are the original Negroid of the world. Their physical characteristics are black skin colour, medium stature, broad nose, thick everted lips and wooly coarse hair.

(ii) Negroids are mainly found in African continent, West Indies, Malaysia, Philippines, Andaman Islands and also in some South-East Asian countries.

(iii) Though this type is the most primitive race today there is hardly pure existence. For example, Bantu and Bushman of South and Central Africa exhibit mixed character.

(2) Caucasoids :

(i) Caucasoids are found mainly in Europe and along the Northern belt of Asia Minor, Afghanistan, Iran to Baluchistan and northern India.

(ii) They are white or red coloured, big heighted, straight haired and blue, green and brown eyed.

(iii) Causcasoids are classified into sub-groups by Hobble and Smith and they are :

(a) Nordic :

(i) The characteristics of this type are fair complexions, tall height, long skulls, mentally superior, inventive and energetic.

(ii) They are dolicocephalic with average height more than 173 cm. Northern European and British belong to this group.

(b) Mediterranean :

(i) This type of people bear dark weavy hair, medium height, brown eyed, long skulls and olive complexion. Average height ranges between 160 - 162 cm.

(ii) They are short tempered, artistic, poetic and musical. Mediterranean Coastlands, Spain, Portugal, Greece and from Italy to India belong to this group.

(c) Alpine :

(i) The people are of short stature, dark hair, sallow complexion and brown eyed belong to this group.

(ii) Average height is 173 cm and mentally they are peace loving, patient and hard workers.

(iii) Alpine regions in Eastern and Central Europe are the homeland of this type of people.

(3) Mongoloid : Refer to point 2.2.1 B (b).

(4) The Australoids : The tribals of Australia who are known as Australian black fellows are Australoids. They are the original inhabitants of Australia.

(5) Capoid : Bushman and *Hottentots* of South Africa belong to this group. They are brownish yellow colour.

(II) Classification based on Physical Traits :

(i) Stature : The average stature of the world population is 165 cm. Whereas no human group is less than 148 cm in stature. The Bushman, the Pygmies and other Negrito people are human dwarfs (148 - 158 cms.) Nordics have high stature (169 + cm).

(ii) Cephalic Index :

$$\text{Cephalic Index} = \frac{\text{Breadth of the Head} \times 100}{\text{Length of the head}}$$

If the cephalic index is less than 75, the race is termed as Dolichocephalic whereas if it is more than 80 it is called Brachysephalic. If its value lies between 75-80, the race is known as Mesocephalic. The orbito = cephalic index refers to the arch or flatness of the head.

(a) Less than 58% - Platycephalic

(b) 58-63% - Orthocephalic

(c) 63 + % - Hyplicephalic

(iii) Nasal Index : It refers to the ratio between the length and breadth of the nose :

(a) Less than 75% - Leptorrhine

(b) 75-85 - Mesorrhine

(c) 85+ % - Platgrhtine

(iv) Hair Structure : Haddon based his classification on hair structure as follows :

(a) Wooly or Frizy Hair (Ulotrichi) : Negritos and Negroids

(b) Straight hair (Leiotrichi) : Mongoloids, Polynesians and Amerinds.

(c) Wavy or curly hair (Cymotrichi) : Caucasoids, Pre-dravidian and Australoids.

(v) Skin Colour : The colour of the skin particularly that of the eye is considered an important discernible trait. The specific colour associated with three major races of mankind by Cuvier are :

(a) Caucasoids : white
(b) Mongoloids : yellow
(c) Negroids : Black

(vi) Prognathism : It refers to the projection of the jaws. This is particularly true of the Negroids who are noted for pronounced prognathism. The Nordics have virtually no prognathism.

(vii) Cranial Capacity : The cranial capacity of the skull is also a criteria for racial classification, however, it can be measured for the dead only. It is estimated that modern man has an average cranial capacity of 1450 c.c.

(viii) Eye-orbital Index : The ratio of the breadth and the length of the eye is called eye-orbital index. "It is 80 for the Negroid, 85-87 for the Australiod and 89-95 for the Mongoloid.

(III) Classification of Indian Races : The large physical dimension exhibits a variety of human races throughout all over India. Here the highest grade of civilization to the lowest are found side by side. The diverse anthropological character of the prehistoric races is still observed among some of the aboriginal tribes of India. Today, India bears a greatest variety of race in the world. Risley, Hutton, Haddon and Prof. B. S. Guha attempted to classify the races of India.

(A) Risley's Classification : According to Risley, there are 7 types of races in the Indian sub-continent. His divisions are :

(i) The Turko Iranian - This type is exclusively found in Baluchistan and the North-Western frontier province. Its leading characteristics are the head is broad, the mean indices ranging from 80 in the Baloch of the Baluchistan to 85 in the Hazara of Afghanistan.

(ii) The Indo- Aryan Type : This type predominante in Rajasthan, Punjab and the Kashmir valley. According to Risley, the Indo-Aryans have the highest stature recorded in India, ranging from 174.8 cm in the Rajput to 165.8 cm.

(iii) The Seytho-Dravidian Type - This type occurs in the Western belt of our country extending from Gujarat to Coorg now in Karnataka. The mean stature of this type varies from 160 cm. to 168.7 cm.

(iv) The Aryo-Dravidian Type : According to Risley, the Aryo-Dravidian type or Hindustani type extends from the eastern Punjab to the southern extremely of Bihar. The mean stature of the Aryo-Dravidians ranges from 166 cm. in the Brahmans and Bhumihars to 159 cm.

(v) The Mongolo-Dravidian - The Gangetic Plain is the main homeland of this type of racial people. It also extends to the Himalayas in the north, Assam in the east and to a major part of Orissa. The stature varies from 167 cm in the Brahmans of West Bengal to 159 in the Kochh of the Sub-Himalayan region.

(vi) The Mongoloid Type : According to Risley, on its Northern and Eastern frontier India marches with the great Mongoloid region of the earth. The prevalent head form is broad but the mean indices show some remarkable departures from this type. In the larger groups the mean nasal index ranges from 67.2 for the Lepchas to 84.5 for the Chakmas and 86.3 for the Khasis; the Tibetans (73.9) and the Murmis (75.4) falling between these extremes.

(vii) The Dravidian Type - The Dravidian race, the most primitive of the Indian type occupies the oldest geological formation in India known as Deccan Plateau, Vindhyas. The characteristics of this type is remarkably uniform and distinctive. The mean stature ranges from 170 cm in the Shanans in Tirumelvelli to 153 cm in the Palaiyas of Kerala and individual measurements vary from 182.8 cm in the former group to 143.4 cm in the latter.

(B) Haddon's Classification : A. C. Haddon classified the Indian races into three groups sub-divided into eight races on the basis of geographical location.

(i) The Himalayan Region : In the Himalayan region, some typical type of races are noticed and they are as follows :

(a) Indo-Aryan : Kanets of the valley region of Kulu and some Nepalese are the representatives of this type. Fair complexion, dark eyes, tall stature and narrow nose are the specific features of these people.

(b) Mongoloid : The North-East frontier region is the main occupied lands of Mongoloid. The full complex of these features is met with most frequently in Himalayan slopes amongst the Lepchas, Garo, Khasi, Naga, Daffia etc. Some Dravidian features are also dominant in Assam and these elements have come from the southern regions where the Dravidians are very dominant.

(ii) The Indo-Gangetic Plain : This type of race is prevailed in the Kashmir valley, Punjab and in Rajputana. Jat and Rajput with light brown skin, tall stature, well developed forehead, long narrow face and sharp nose are the typical examples of this type.

(iii) The Deccan : According to Haddon following racial elements are found in the Deccan :

(a) Negrito : The Mincoi people of the Andaman and Nicobar Islands, "were preserved upto recent times by their isolation in islands about 350 kms from the mainland. Negrito features are met with particularly amongst the Andaman Islands and most probably the Uralis of Nilgiri Hills, Kadars of Cochin on Kerala, Pullayanas of Palni Hills etc.

(b) Pre-Dravidian : The jungles of the Deccan Plateau represent very primitive types of low culture of certain groups which are known according to Haddon as Pre-Dravidian.

(c) Dravidians : This type is found in Karnataka, Kerala and Nilgiri with Deshastha Brahman, Tamil Sudra, Tamil Brahman, Nambudiri Brahmans and Nayar of Malabar forming the greatest percentage of this type.

(d) Western Brachycephals : The Nagar Brahman of south western India represented this type. It is a zone of relatively broad headed people. The western Brachycephals extend from Gujarat to Karnataka, along the Western coastal area of India.

(e) Southern Brachycephals : This type is represented by the Priyan of Tamil and Prava of Tirunelveli.

(C) Hutton's Classification : Dr. Hutton has suggested the following classifications of the ethnic elements in India :

(i) **Negrito :** According to Hutton, the people of the Negrito race were the earliest people of India in Southern India. Similar races also appear in some inaccessible areas between Assam and Myanmar whose typical characteristics is a dwarfish stature and frizzly hair.

(ii) **Proto-Australoid :** Proto-Austroloid came from the East Mediterranean area. "The Veddahs, Malavedahs, Iruals, Sholages are the true representative of this type.

(iii) **Early Mediterranean :** According to Dr. Hutton, "Northern India was occupied by the Mediterranean race, before the Armenoid stock began to mingle with them, and it is possible that they were connected with the Indonesian race.

(iv) **Civilized Mediterranean :** This type is responsible for the development of Indus valley civilization and also known as Dravidians in India.

(v) **Alpine :** Dr. Hutton defines, "*The race appears to have been at any rate partly responsible for the highly developed civilization of ancient Mesopotamia and Asia Minor and in both areas it has every where mingled with the Mediterranean race which it found in occupation.*"

(vi) **Armenoides :** This type is developed due to the mixture of hook shaped Mediterranean & Brachycephalic Alpines. The characteristics of these people are sugar loaf heaf form, convex nose with fleshy depressed tip and flaring wings.

(vii) **Nordic :** Hutton thinks that Nordic occupied North-Western India from the beginning of the fourth millennium BC and they are supposed to have brought the Sanskrit language in India.

(viii) **Mongoloid :** According to Hutton, " The race movement of Mongolians southwards still continued among to the Kochin tribe while the Kuki- Chin tribes have barely settled down after reaching the Bay of Bengal and starting to work northwards again on the Assam side of the dividing ranges. The bulk of Myanmar in any case is primarily Mongoloid.

(D) Dr. Guha's Classification : Dr. Guha divided Indian races into six main groups and then sub-divided them into thirteen groups. They are as follows :

(i) Negrito : Kadars are the true representative of this type, Dr. Guha writes, " whatever might have been the original type, there can be at any rate no doubt that this was Negrito".

(ii) The Proto-Australoid : Mundas, Kols etc. are the examples of this type, whose skin colour is dark brown or black, short stature and fleshy everted lips.

(iii) Mongoloid : Short to medium stature, epicanthic eyefold, flat nose and face. This type is sub-divided into :

(A) Pale - Mongoloid : Dark brown to black skin colour, medium nose, oblique eye sight and cheek bones are the main features.

(a) Long - headed type : The semi Naga is the true representative of this type.

(b) Broad-headed type : The people are broad headed with dark skin and flat face.

(B) Tibeto Mongoloid : Physically broad headed with dark skin, obliquity of eyelites and broad nose are the characteristics of the people of Sikkim and Bhutan.

(iv) Mediterranean : Their physical features are : A long head, short to medium statured, brown skinned element prominant in the upper classes of north India, and to some extent the Punjab people are adulated Mediterranean type. They have been sub-divided into :

(a) Pale Mediterranean : Tamil and Telegu Brahmans are the examples of this type.

(b) Mediterranean : Kashmiri, Rajputs, Maratha and Uttar Pradesh Brahmans are the typical examples of this type.

(c) Oriental Type : The people of Western Uttar Pradesh, Punjab and Rajasthan are the representatives of this type.

(v) The Nordic : Bengalis with tall stature, fair skin colour, long head and narrow nose are the representatives of this type.

(vi) Alpo - Denaric : They further sub-divided into :

(a) Alpinoid : Kayasthas of Bengal, Bania of Gujarat and Kathis of Saurashtra are the representatives of their group.

(b) Dinaric : The people of this group are found in Kerala and Orissa.

(c) Armenoid : The characteristics of this group are tall stature, fair skin colour, long head and narrow nose.

2.3 Bases of Human Race

- In biology, race can be defined as a "geographically bounded population" showing accentuated genetic differentiation. It is believed that the division of human species into "races" presents a solid biological base.
- The human being feels the need of classifying everything around them. Even though the first classifications of the species are from immemorial times, it is known that the philosophers separated the beings in aerial, terrestrial and aquatic domains or whether they are useful or hazardous to humans.
- In the biological classification forwarded by Linneaus, the species are separated in categories, going from the most broad (rein) until the most specific (species).
- The subdivision of different populations of a species is denominated subspecies, correct designation of what we call "race".
- This concept was first introduced to human populations by the French biologist Buffon.
- The term "race" has several meanings in biology. According to Mayr, race is a sympatric population, not interrelating, that differs in its biologic characteristics, but it does not differ in morphologic characteristics.
- Futuyma states that race is a vague and meaningless term, for a set of populations occupying a particular region that differ in one or more characteristics from populations elsewhere, frequently equivalent to subspecies.

- Although the race concept in some few cases, be used to show inequities between human groups, the utilization of this concept in medical sciences can contribute to ideas of biologic determinism and complicate diseases diagnosis.
- There is a belief that the distinction of human being has a solid base in biologic evidences.
- A partial isolation allowed the beginning of the differentiation of the species. But after the beginning of the Great European Navigations, any type of isolation was capable to be broken. With the innovation and increase of the transports this possibility reached significant levels. Besides, trying to apply only geographic criteria for the designation of human races is not sufficient because, as stated Cartmill if "black", "white", "asiatic" and amerindians individuals that are born in the same place are different by the racial point of view, so the races are not distinct geographically.
- There is not a specific criteria that can guarantee to populations the designation of race, which is taking lots of systems to propose the abandon of the term. Applied to human beings, this term corresponds to an arbitrary system of visual classification that does not separate distinct populations.
- 'Race' shows characteristic of convenience, which is used when there is the need to distinguish populations, which makes different criteria to be used by different classifying agents.
- Several characteristics and genetic polymorphisms show different geographic patterns with the possibility of several combinations to distinguish one population from another.
- The categarization of human beings depends on who and where the evaluation is done. Anthropologists are not from the elite and that had a social origin less privileged tend to be more receptive to the position of non existence of races than their colleagues from elite institutions.

- In England, "Asiatics" correspond to people that come from India, Pakistan and Bangladesh, whereas in the United States, it describes people from Pacific Islands, China and Japan.
- The definition of some races can change with the time. In the Unites States, Mexicans were considered "white" during the period of 1940 and 1950, being designated as "hispanics".
- Frequently the criteria utilized for the racial classification is not efficient. Generally used external morphologic feature is not very representative genetically.
- The environment and age are factors extremely important in the definition of the color of a person which turns very difficult to associate a certain phenotype to a genotype. The interaction with the environment is individual, depends on the history of life of each person, despite being similar to individuals inhabiting the same geographic region.
- Race is a typological concept and is based upon ideal, non-existent types in the nature. Being a static concept, based upon fixed types, race cannot explain the complex changes of structures in the biologic human variation. The biological human variation, as well as of the other species is continuous, complex and changeable.
- The human beings show a modest level of genetic differentiation and this level of differentiation is below from what is conventionally written of what separate races.
- Only recently we can test the existence of races in more precise biological terms, with the advance of genetics and molecular biology.
- The results of extensive genetic studies of several human populations from different continents show the fragility of the concept of race, because it was verified that the human diversity was higher inside the "racial" or geographic groups than among them.

- Lewontin, analyzing populations from distinct continents, concluded that 85% of the human genetic diversity occurred inside the populations or races.
- In 1980, studying the populations of Europe, Africa, Asia, America and Oceania, Latter verified that the diversity inside the populations was nearly 84%, among populations of one group 6% and only 10% among the geographic groups. Other studies with several populations and different markers had the same conclusion.

2.4 Griffith Taylor's Theory of Human Race

- Thomas Griffith (1 December 1880 – 5 November 1963) was an English geographer, anthropologist and world explorer.
- Taylor was the leader of the successful geological team, responsible for the first maps and geological interpretations of significant areas of Antarctica.
- Taylor was awarded the King's Polar medal and made a fellow of the Royal Geographical Society of London.
- Taylor's physiographical and geomorphological Antarctic research earned him a doctorate (D.Sc) from the University of Sydney in 1916.
- He was made Associate Professor of Geography in 1921 becoming the founding head of the Department of Geography at the university.
- Taylor wrote many books about the effects of the environment in shaping race. He also wrote extensively about migration of the races.
- According to Taylor "The fittest tribes evolve and survive in the most stimulating regions; i.e., where living is not so hard as to stunt mental development, and not so easy as to encourage sloth and loss of initiative. The least fit are ultimately crowded out into the deserts, the tropical jungles, or the rugged mountains."
- With regard to anthropology, Taylor looks at records of hair texture and size, nose size, ear size, cephalic indices, skin colour, and height.

- The most suitable parts of the world for habitation, according to Taylor are Europe, Western Siberia, the Americas and Eastern China.
- Taylor was the author of some 20 books and 200 scientific articles.

The Theory

- Griffith Taylor, a recognised geographer of 20 century, who founded a theory known as "Migration Zone Theory of Race Evolution'. To establish his theory, Taylor first developed five main principles of race evolution and they are as follows :

(i) According to Taylor, "*the most primitive race was found pushed to the periphery*" i.e. in Tasmania, Cape Colony, Greenland and Brazil. This is the first principle.

(ii) The second principle said that the last evolved races are found in the centre, where stimuli leading to evolution have been greatest throughout the ages.

(iii) The third principle of race evolution is that, "*where the racial evolution has progressed farthest, the burried strata of more primitive tribes will be most numerous.*"

(iv) In the fourth priciple, Taylor described "the order of evolution is the same, whether we move outwards from the centre of evolution across the zones or downwards at the centre of evolution through the strata."

(v) According to the fifth principle, "primitive races are found alive precisely where they did not originate." Dr. Taylor said, "The evidence in Europe, Africa, South Asia and Australia shows an age long centrifugal movement from Central Asia. American evidence is more complex but the same kind".

Taylor also defined seven different stratas of human life according to their existence in the world and it is :

(i) The Neanderthal who was the earliest and most primitive man in the earth. This type is traced almost to various parts in southern, western and central Europe. This is the first stratum.

(ii) The Negrito race is graded by Taylor in the second stratum.

(iii) Negroid is the third stratum. In the end of the Paleolithic age, these would have been quite abundant. Their existence is universal through Africa to Melanesia.

(iv) Australoid, the fourth stratum has a world wide existence. This type was found in Australia, Indonesia, South-East Asia and in South India.

(v) The fifth stratum labelled as Mediterranean has an affiliation with the Pro-magnon folk of super Paleolithic age. The broad faces and narrow skulls which are characterising physical features found in the Cannary Isles and Eskimos of Greenland.

- Most of the Amerinds are also the Pro-magnon type. The people of this category once occupied the whole territory of the Alpine region and developed Paleolithic and Neolithic civilization throughout the world.

(vi) Nordics represent the sixth stratum, which according to Taylor is a specialised upper zone of Mediterranean. It has a typical occurrence in North-West Europe, but also found from Turkistan to northern Japan i.e. Venessi river basin, Tarim Basin, southern Persia and the Atlas Mountain.

(vii) Alpine or Mongolian is the last stratum. According to many geographers, the Caucasians and the Mongolians are the two distinct races of this type.

- But Taylor did not agree to such distinction because he said that the reasons for this division are not satisfactory. According to him, slantness of eyes also occurs among other races like Mongolians and cheek bones are also prominent in some parts of Scotland.
- So it is difficult to draw a demarcatory line between European Alpines and the Asiatic Mongoloids. This is the top stratum and according to the law of geographical superimposition they are the last evolved.

2.5 Pure and Mix Races

"A race is a biological inbreed group possessing a distinctive combination of physical traits that tend to breed true from generation to generation."

According to **A. L. Kroeber**, *"Race is a human group united by heredity, a breed or sub-species".*

Wellice defined, *"Race is a human group with homogeneous hereditary characters or biological traits".*

Generally Accepted Divisions : (i) Caucasoid (European), (ii) Negroid (African), (iii) Mongoloid (Asiatic or Oriental, (iv) Indic (Hindu), (v) Australoid (Australians), (vi) Polynesians, (vii) Melanesians (viii) Micronesians (sometimes these three are classed as Oceanic) and American Indian.

Pure Race and Mixed Race :

(i) It is clear from the analysis of physical traits of various racial groups that no single group of human beings has a monopoly of any single trait, or cluster of traits.

(ii) With the years, it has become increasingly evident that the outstanding factor in the study of physical types is 'variability'. The intermingling of blood has taken place to the extent that there is hardly any 'pure race', even in the remotest and isolated areas of the world. There is no evidence of the existence of so-called 'pure' races.

(iii) With regard to race mixture, the evidence points to the fact that human hybridization has been going on for an indefinite but considerable time. Indeed one of the processes of race formation and race extinction or absorption is by means of hybridization between races.

(iv) Due to continuous migration, at present, the Caucasoid sub-races have submerged the aboriginals and native people in North America, South America and Oceania. Similar is the case in Asia, Africa and the islands of the Pacific, Indian and Arctic Oceans.

(v) Fast mobility of man has led to intermingling of blood and cross-breeding and this in its turn has made the idea of 'Pure race' as futile. At present admixture is probable even in the short span, that racial purity becomes a meaningless term. The anthropological ideas discussed above are scientific but limited, the categories are to a large extent abstract and very difficult to apply to small groups of people.

The Aryan Race Concept :

The Aryan race is a historical race concept which emerged in the period of the late 19th century and mid-20th century to describe people of Indo-European heritage as a racial grouping.

- The original speakers of the Indo-European languages and their descendants up to the present day constitute a distinctive race or subrace of the Caucasian race according to this concept.
- The term *Aryan* has generally been used to describe the Proto-Indo-Iranian language root **arya* which was the ethnonym the Indo-Iranians adopted to describe Aryans.
- The term Indo-Aryan is still commonly used to describe the Indic half of the Indo-Iranian languages, i.e., the family that includes Sanskrit and modern languages such as Hindi-Urdu, Bengali, Punjabi, Gujarati, Romani, Kashmiri, Sinhalese and Marathi.
- Max Muller is often identified as the first writer to mention an "Aryan race" in English.
- While the "Aryan race" theory remained popular, particularly in Germany, some authors opposed it.
- Müller's concept of Aryan was later construed to imply a biologically distinct sub-group of humanity, by writers such as Arthur de Gobineau, who argued that the Aryans represented a superior branch of humanity.
- By the late 19th century the steppe theory of Indo-European origins was challenged by a view that the Indo-Europeans originated in ancient Germany or Scandinavia – or at least that in

those countries the original Indo-European ethnicity had been preserved.

- In the 1944 edition of Rand McNally's *World Atlas*, the Aryan race is depicted as one of the ten major racial groupings of mankind.

Multiracial

- Multiracial is defined as made up of or relating to people of many races.
- Individuals of multiracial backgrounds make up a significant portion of the population in many parts of the world. In North America, studies have found that the multiracial population is continuing to grow.

In the United States

- The revised OMB standards identify a minimum of five racial categories: White; Black or African American; American Indian and Alaska Native; Asian; and Native Hawaiian and Other Pacific Islander.

Africa

North Africa and Middle East

- In North Africa, a large number of multiracial communities exist. Among these are the Haratin oasis-dwellers of Saharan southern Morocco, Algeria and Mauritania.
- Arab and Ottoman slave traders sold slaves in large numbers throughout the Persian Gulf, Anatolia, Central Asia and the Arab world and communities originated from these slaves who can be found throughout these regions.

Madagascar

- Almost the complete population of Madagascar is an admixture of South East Asian (Indonesian) primarily from Borneo and Bantu-speaking settlers primarily from Mozambique.

South Africa

- Multiracial South Africans are known as *Coloureds*. According to the 2016 South African Census, they are the second largest minority (8.8%) after white South Africans (8.1%).

Asia

Central Asia

- Many Central Asian populations are a mixture of various peoples such as Mongols, Turkics, and Iranians. The Mongol invasion of Central Asia in the 13th century resulted in intermarriage and assimilation.
- Genetic studies show that Central Asian Turkic people and Hazara are a mixture of Northeast Asians and Indo-European people.
- Caucasian ancestry is prevalent in almost all central Asian Turkic people. Kazakhs, Hazara, Karakalpaks.

India

- Anglo-Indians are a Eurasian mix which originated in India during the Colonial rule beginning with the French, Dutch, Portuguese and other Europeans during the British Raj in India.
- The estimated population of Anglo-Indians is 600,000 globally with the majority living in India and the UK.
- Article 366(2) of the Indian Constitution defines Anglo-Indian as an Anglo-Indian means a person whose father or any of whose other male progenitors in the male line is or was of European descent but who is domiciled within the territory of India and is or was born within such territory of parents habitually resident therein and not established there for temporary purposes only;
- Goans are mixture of Indo-Aryan, Eurasian and Luso-Asians ancestries, with many descendants of the Portuguese, who had influence on Goa for over 450 years.

Myanmar (Burma)

- Myanmar formerly known as Burma was a British colony, from 1826 until 1948. Many European groups competed for control of the country before the British arrived.
- Intermarriage and mixed-relationships between these foreign settlers and merchants with the local Burmese population and between British colonists and the Burmese created a local Eurasian population, known as the Anglo-Burmese.

- This group dominated colonial society through the early years of independence. Most Anglo-Burmese now reside primarily in Australia, New Zealand and the UK.

Philippines

- This country was a Spanish colony for nearly four centuries or 333 years, and by the United States for 46 years. This is the cause of many mixed race Filipinos of Spanish Filipino and Philippine-American descent.
- In the United States, intermarriage among Filipinos with other races is common. They have the largest number of interracial marriages among Asian immigrant groups, as documented in California.

Singapore and Malaysia

- In Singapore and Malaysia the majority of inter-ethnic marriages are between Chinese and Indians. The offsprings of such marriages are informally known as "Chindian", though the Malaysian government only classifies them by their father's ethnicity.
- The Chitty people, in Singapore and the Malacca state of Malaysia, are Tamils with considerable Malay descent.
- In the East Malaysian states of Sabah and Sarawak, there have been many incidents of intermarriage between Chinese and native tribes such as the Murut and Dusun in Sabah, and the Iban and Bisaya in Sarawak.

Sri Lanka

- The most notable mixed-race group are the Sri Lankan Moors, who trace their ancestry from Arab traders who settled on the island and intermarried with local women.
- The 'Burghers' are a Eurasian ethnic group, consisting for the most part of male-line descendants of European colonists from the 16th to 20th centuries (mostly Portuguese, Dutch, German and British) and local women, with some minorities of Swedish, Norwegian, French and Irish.

- The Sri Lanka 'Kaffirs' are an ethnic group partly descended from 16th century Portuguese traders and the African slaves who were brought by them.

Vietnam

- Under terms of the Geneva Accords of 1954, departing French troops took thousands of Vietnamese wives and children with them after the First Indochina War. Some 100,000 Eurasians stayed in Vietnam, after independence from French rule.

Europe

United Kingdom

- *The Sunday Times* reported that "Britain has the highest rate of interracial relationships in the world" and certainly the UK has the highest rate in the European Union.
- In the United Kingdom, many multiracial people have Caribbean, African or Asian heritage.

North America

Canada

- The most frequent combinations were *multiple visible minorities* (for example, people of mixed black and South Asian heritage form the majority), followed closely by *white-black, white-Chinese, white-Arab* and many other smaller mixes.
- 1.2% of Canadians officially are Métis (descendants of a historical population who were partially Aboriginal also called "Indian" or "Native" and European, particularly English, Scottish, Irish and French ethnic groups). Although listed as a single "race" in Canada, the Métis are therefore multiracial.

United States

- Multiracial Americans officially numbered 6.1 million in 2006, or 2.0% of the population. According to the Census Bureau, as of 2002, over 75% of all African Americans had multiracial ancestries usually Native American.
- Many mixed raced Americans use the term *biracial*. The US has a growing multiracial identity movement, reflective of a desire by people to claim their full identities.

- The United States is one of the most racially diverse countries in the world. Americans are mostly multi-ethnic descendants of various immigrant nationalities culturally distinct in their former countries.

Oceania

Fiji

- Fiji has long been a multi-ethnic country, with a vast majority of people having multi-racial heritages. The indigenous Fijians are of mixed Melanesian and Polynesian ancestry, resulting from years of migration of islanders from various places mixing with each other.
- Over the years, particularly in the sugar cane-growing regions of Western Viti Levu and parts of Vanua Levu, Indo-Fijians and Indigenous Fijians have mixed. Others have Chinese/Fijian ancestry, Indo-Fijian/Samoan or Rotuman ancestry and European / Fijian ancestry (often called "part Fijians").

South America and the Caribbean

- Mestizo is the common word used to describe multiracial people in Latin America, especially people with Native American and Spanish or other European ancestry.
- Trinidad and Tobago, Guyana and Suriname claim the highest populations of mixtures such known locally as *douglas*.
- In addition to mixed African and Indian heritage, inhabitants of Trinidad and Tobago can also have any combination of Amerindian, Latino, European, Chinese, Arab and Jewish heritage.

Brazil

- The most common multiracial groups are between European and African and Amerindian and European. But there are also African and Amerindian and East Asian and European/other. All groups are more or less found throughout the whole country.
- Brazilian multiracials with the following three origins, Amerindian, European and African, make up the majority.

POINTS TO REMEMBER

- There is no such evidence to prove when the first man appeared on the earth and at which place he was born.
- Man is a primate or one of the highest group of mammals.
- A Race is a biological group possessing a distinctive combination of physical traits that tend to breed true from generation to generation.
- The Races of the world are classified into five principle classes by some anthropologists : (i) The Negroid (ii) Caucasoid, (iii) Mongoloid, (iv) The Australoids (v) Capoid.
- **Risleys's classification** of races in the Indian sub-continent : (i) The Turko-Iranian (ii) The Indo-Aryan group, (iii) The Seytho-Dravidian type (iv) The Aryo-Dravidian type, (v) Mongolo-Dravidian, (vi) The Mongoloid type, (vii) The Dravidian type.
- Haddon's classification of Indian races :

(i) The Himalayan Region : (a) Indo-Aryan, (b) Mongoloid,

(ii) The Indo Gangetic Plains,

(iii) The Deccan- (a) Negrito, (b) Pre-Dravidian, (c) Dravidians, (d) Western Brachycephals, (e) Southern Brachycephals.

- Hutton's Classification : (a) Negrito, (b) Proto-Australoid, (c) Early, Mediterranean, (d) Civilized Mediterranean, (e) Alpine, (f) Armenoids, (g) Nordic (h) Mongoloid.
- Dr. Guha's classification : (a) Negrito, (b) The Proto-Australoid, (c) Mongoloid, (d) Mediterranean, (e) The Nordic Alpo Denaric.
- Thomas Griffith was an English geographer, anthropologist and world explorer. He forwarded 'Migration zone theory of Race evolution.
- Max Muller is often identified as the first writer to mention an "Aryan Race" in English.
- Multiracial is defined as made up of or relating to people of many races.

✧ QUESTIONS ✧

Q. I : Answer the following Questions in Detail :

(1) *What are the various stages of Human Evolution ?*

(2) *Give the meaning and Definition of Human Race.*

(3) *What are the five principle classes of races in the world ?*

(4) *How classification of humans has been done on the basis of Physical traits ?*

(5) *What are the Bases of Human Race ?*

(6) *What is the theory of Race evolution by Griffith Taylor ?*

(7) *Compare between Mixed and Pure Races.*

Q. II : Write short notes :

(1) *Homosapiens*

(2) *Risley classification*

(3) *Haddon's classification*

(4) *Hutton's classification*

(5) *Griffith Taylor*

(6) *Aryan Race*

(7) *Multiracialism*

✻ ✻ ✻

UNIT – 3

STUDY OF INDIAN TRIBES

SYNOPSIS

INTRODUCTION

The Indian Tribes own their own unique personal identity as '*Adivasi*' having their own language, religion, festivals, cuisine, dance and music. They also have a significantly contrasting patriarchal and matriarchal society.

The total number of tribal groups in India, exceeds more than 500 and comprises approximately 12% of the total Indian population. The habitats of the tribal community in India stretches from the remote villages of the Indian Himalayan region to southern distant corner of North East India to deserts of Rajasthan. The tribal population in India covers approximately 15% of the country and the majority are found in central India.

The tribal art forms a unique alley in the Indian handicraft industry. There are festivals like the 'Hornbill' festival in Nagaland, '*Keshai Khaity*' festival in Assam, '*Disum Sendra*' in West Bengal, '*Bhagoria Haat*' festival in Madhya Pradesh, '*Baneshwar Fair*' in Rajasthan, '*Sammakka Saralamma Jatra*' in Andhra Pradesh, '*Kokan Festival*' in Maharashtra, and '*Thulappathu*' festival in Kerala. In Himachal Pradesh you will find the Gurjar, Gaddi, Pangwala and Bodh tribes. Moing deep into the mystic mountains of Meghalaya you will meet the Khasi, Garo and Jaintia tribes. Travelling to the archipelago of Andaman you will come across the Jarawa tribes and wheeling from the backwaters of Kerala to the verdure of Karnataka, experience the harmony of the Paniyar, Kurichyar, Kattunaikkar, Mullukkurumar, Adiyar, Kanduvadiyar, Thachanadar, Kanaladi, Soliga, Siddis and more.

Their lifestyle is completely different from the rest of the world. They are still competing to get adjusted with the modern trend. Each tribe has its own respective culture - food, festival, dance, music, religion and language.

"*Adivasi*' is the comprehensive term for tribes in the Indian subcontinent, who are considered indigenous to places (i.e., forests) within India wherein they live, either as foragers or as tribalistic sedentary communities. The term is also used for ethnic minorities, such as Chakmas of Bangladesh, Tharus of Nepal and Bhills of Pakistan.

They consists of a substantial minority population of India ,Nepal and a minority group of the Sri Lankan society called the Vedda, making up 8.6% of India's population, or 104 million people, according to the 2011 census, and a large percentage of the Nepalese population. Tribal societies are prominent in states of Andhra Pradesh, Chhattisgarh, Gujarat, Jharkhand, Madhya Pradesh, Odisha, Maharashtra, West Bengal, and Northeast India, and the Andaman and Nicobar Islands.

The present-day tribals formed after the decline of the Indus Valley Civilisation, harboring various degrees of ancestry from ancient hunter-gatherers, Indo-Aryan, and Austroasiatic and Tibeto-Burman language speakers. There are five linguistic groupings, Andamanese; Austro-Asiatic; Dravidian; Indo - Aryan; Sino-Tibetan; and Kra-Dai.

3.1 Regional distribution of Tribes in India

Major Tribes in India: State-wise compilation:

Tribe (Meaning) A tribe is a social division in a traditional society consisting of families linked by social, economic, religious, or blood ties, with a common culture and dialect.

- A tribe has certain qualities and characteristics that make it a unique cultural, social, and political entity.

Tribes in India

- The constitution of India has recognized tribal communities in India under 'Schedule 5' of the constitution and are known as 'Scheduled Tribes'. There are around 645 tribes in India.
- Population of Scheduled Tribes is 84,326,240 as per the Census 2001 which accounts for 8.2% of the total population of country.
- Madhya Pradesh, Maharastra, Orissa, Gujarat, Rajasthan, Jharkhand, Chhattisgarh, Andhra Pradesh, West Bengal, and Karnataka are the state having largest number of Scheduled Tribes

  These states account for 83.2% of the total Scheduled Tribe population of the country.
- Assam, Meghalaya, Nagaland, Jammu & Kashmir, Tripura, Mizoram, Bihar, Manipur, Arunachal Pradesh, and Tamil Nadu, account for another 15.3% of the total Scheduled Tribe population.
- The scheduled Tribes in India form the largest percentage of the total population in Lakshadweep and Mizoram followed by Nagaland and Meghalaya.
- Madhya Pradesh has the maximum number of scheduled Tribes followed by Bihar.
- There are no Scheduled Tribes in Punjab, Delhi, Chandigarh, Pondicherry, Haryana.
- Allocation of seats for Scheduled Tribes in the Lok Sabha are made on the basis of proportion of Scheduled Tribes in the State concerned to that of the total population
- For Scheduled Tribes, 47 seats are reserved in Lok Sabha.
- Article 366 (25) defined scheduled tribes as "such tribes or tribal communities or parts of or groups within such tribes or tribal communities as are deemed under Article 342 to be Scheduled Tribes for the purposes of this constitution".

Article 342 in the Constitution of India 1949

Scheduled Tribes

(1) The President may with respect to any State or Union territory, and where it is a State, after consultation with the Governor thereof, by public notification, specify the tribes or tribal communities or parts of or groups within tribes or tribal communities which shall for the purposes of this Constitution be deemed to be Scheduled Tribes in relation to that State or Union territory, as the case may be

(2) **Parliament** may by law include in or exclude from the list of Scheduled Tribes specified in a notification issued under clause (1) any tribe or tribal community or part of or group within any tribe or tribal community, but save as aforesaid a notification issued under the said clause shall not be varied by any subsequent notification.

Ministry of Tribal Affairs

- Ministry of Tribal Affairs is in charge for the complete development of the scheduled tribes in India. This Ministry established in 1999 after the bifurcation of Ministry of Social Justice and Empowerment with the objective of adopting more focused approach on the integrated socio-economic development of the Scheduled Tribes (STs), who are the most underprivileged of the Indian Society.
- With regard to programmes of development of these communities policy, planning, monitoring, etc. including coordination will be the responsibility of the concerned Central Ministries/ Departments, State Governments and Union Territory Administrations. Each Central Ministry/Department will be the nodal Ministry or Department concerning its sector.
- Before the formation of the Ministry, tribal affairs were handled by different Ministries as follows:

(i) As a Division of the Ministry of Home Affairs named as 'Tribal Division' (independence up to September, 1985).

(ii) Ministry of Welfare (September 1985 to May 1998).

(iii) Ministry of Social Justice & Empowerment from (May 1998 to September 1999).

National Commission for Scheduled Tribes (NCST)

- The National Commission for Scheduled Tribes (NCST) was established by amending Article 338 and inserting a new Article 338A in the Constitution through the Constitution (89th Amendment) Act, 2003. By this amendment, the erstwhile National Commission for Scheduled Castes and Scheduled Tribes was replaced by two separate Commissions namely-

(i) The National Commission for Scheduled Castes (NCSC), and

(ii) The National Commission for Scheduled Tribes (NCST) w.e.f. 19th February, 2004.

The Tribal Sub Plan (TSP) strategy

- The Tribal Sub Plan (TSP) strategy is a Government of India initiative aimed for rapid socio-economic progress of tribal people. Central Ministries/Departments are also required to earmark funds out of their budget for the Tribal Sub-Plan. The National Commission for Scheduled Tribes is vested with the duty to participate and advise in the planning process of socio-economic development of STs, and to evaluate the progress of their development under the Union and any State.

Regional Distribution of Tribes in India

- India is the home to a large number of tribes, who are still untouched by the modern world. There are 461 tribes in India out of which 424 are considered as the Schedule Tribes
- Question is who are tribes or which people belongs to the tribal groups ? In 1960, Chanda Committee determined five standards to include any caste or community in the tribal group.
- These standards include geographical isolation, special culture, characteristics of tribes, backwardness and shyness.

Regional Distribution of Tribes in India

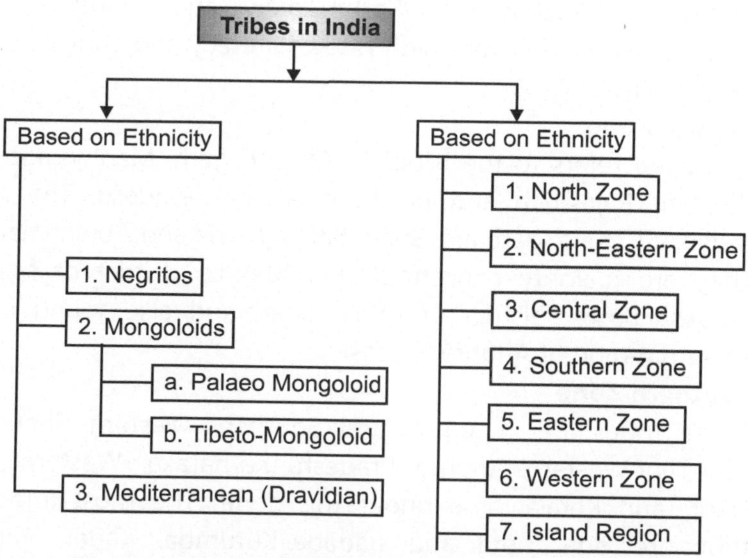

Fig. 3.1 : Regional Distribution of Tribes in India

- India can be divided into seven zones on the basis of distribution and diversity of the tribal population which are given below:

1. **North Zone**

- This zone includes the tribes of the region of Jammu & Kashmir, Himachal Pradesh, Punjab, Uttarakhand, Sub Himalayan Uttar Pradesh, and Bihar. They are Lahul, Lepcha, Bhotia, Tharu, Buxa, Jaunsari, Khampa, Bhoksa, Gujjars and Kanauta and they belong to racial group. The suffer from accessibility, lack of communication, poverty, illiteracy and land alienation.

2. **North-Eastern Zone**

- This zone includes tribes of Assam, Arunachal Pradesh, Nagaland, Manipur, Tripura, Meghalaya and Mizoram. They also have the characteristics of the Mongoloids racial group. The major tribal groups are:

  Nagaland : Naga, Kuki, Mikir and Garo
  Mizoram : Lusai, Kuki, Garo, Khasi, Jayantia and Mikir
  Meghalaya : Garo, Khasi and Jayantia
  Sikkim : Lepcha, Bhutia, Limbu, and Tamang
  Tripura : Chakma, Garo, Khasi, Kuki, Lusai, Liang, and Santhal
  Arunachal Pradesh : Dafla, Khampti, and Singpho
  Manipur : Meities, Pangals, Naga tribes and Kuki
  Asom : Boro, Kachari, Mikir (Karbi), Lalung, and Hajong

  These tribes have a very high rate of literacy and conversions to Christianity.

3. **Central Zone**

- This zone refers to the tribes of Chhattisgarh, Madhya Pradesh, Western Rajasthan and northern Andhra Pradesh. The major tribes of Chhattisgarh are Gond, Baiga, Maria and Abujhamaria.
- They are majority concentrated in Mandla district of Madhya Pradesh, Bastar district of Chhattisgarh and also found in the eastern region of Andhra Pradesh.

4. **Southern Zone**

- These tribes are in Central and Southern Western Ghats. The tribes of Western Andhra Pradesh, Karnataka, Western Tamil Nadu and Kerala come under this zone. The most important tribes are Toda, Kota and Bagada, Kurumba, Kadar, Paniyan, Chenchu, Allar, Nayak and Chetti.

5. Eastern Zone

- The tribes of Jharkhand, West Bengal, Odisha and Bihar come under this zone. Odisha tribes are Juang, Kharia, Khond and Bhumij. The tribes of Jharkhand are Munda, Oraon, Santhal, Ho and Birhor. They speak Kol and Munda languages.

6. Western Zone

- This zone refers to tribes of Chhattisgarh, Madhya Pradesh, Western Rajasthan, and northern Andhra Pradesh. The major tribes of Rajasthan are Bhill, Garasia, Mina, Banjara, Sansi and Saharia; Gujarat are Mahadeokoli, Bali and Dabala; in Madhya Pradesh is Jayanti.

7. Island Region

- It includes the tribes of Andaman & Nicobar and Lakshadweep. The major tribes are Shompen, Onge, Jarawa and Sentinali, who are gradually becoming extinct. They are related to the Negrito racial group. All the racial groups are identified according to their own racial characteristics. These characteristics are the nature and colour of hair, head structure, Nasal index and shape of eyes. However, the racial groups in India are highly mixed.

Geographical Distribution of Tribes in India – Essay :

- The tribes are everywhere in the country. About 2/3 of the total tribal population of the country are found in the five states – Orrisa, Madhya Pradesh, Bihar, Gujarat and Maharashtra.
- The tribes live from the foot-hills of Himalayas to the land tip, of Lakshadweep and from plains of Gujarat to the hills of North-East.
- The peninsular region has Bhills, Gonds, Santhals, Ho, Kols, Kondh, Kharia and Mundas etc. In the North-Eastern region the prominent tribals are Nagas, the Mizos, Mikris and Kukis.

Dr. B. S. Guha has divided the county into three tribal Zones:

1. North and North-Eastern Zone :

- This zone consists of eastern Kashmir, Eastern Punjab, Himachal Pradesh, Northern Uttar Pradesh, Nagaland, Assam etc. The Aka, the Mishmi, the Chulikata and the Naga are some of the tribes of this zone.

2. Central Zone :

- This zone consists of Bihar, Bengal, Southern Uttar Predesh, Southern Rajasthan, Madhya Pradesh and Orissa. The Kondh, the Santhal, the Bhill, the Gond, the Muria and the Baiga are only a few of the large number of tribes of this zone. There is a very high concentration of tribal population in central India. Over 85 per cent of the total tribal population inhabits the eight States in this zone.

3. Southern Zone :

- This zone consists of four Southern States – Andhra Pradesh, Tamil Nadu, Karnataka and Kerala. The Toda, the Chenchu, the Kadar and the Koraga are some of the important tribes of this zone. C. B. Mamoria has added to this list the fourth zone consisting of Andaman and Nicobar Islands.

4. The Small Zone consisting of Andaman and Nicobar Islands :

- There is another isolated zone in the Andaman and Nicobar Island in the Bay of Bengal. The Jarawa, the Andamanese and the Nicobarese are the important tribes of this zone.
- B. K. Roy Burman categories the tribal population of the country into five geographical regions taking territorial, ethnic and socio-cultural relations as criteria.

1. **The North-East India :** Consisting of Assam, NEFA, Nagaland, Manipur and Tripura. Some of the tribes of this area are: the Ahoms, Garos, Khasis, Mizos, Nagas, Kukis, etc.
2. **The sub-Himalayan region** of North and North West India - consisting of Northern Uttar Pradesh and Himachal Pradesh and as a whole. Some tribes of this area are: Gujjars, Bodh, Kinnours, Swanglia, etc.
3. **Central and East India :** Consisting West Bengal, Bihar, Orissa, Madhya Pradesh and Andhra Pradesh. Some tribes of this area: the Santals, Ho, Munda, Oraons, Gonds, Chenchu, Koya, Kolam, etc.
4. **South India :** Consisting Chennai, Kerala and Karnataka. The tribes of this area are Irula, Kurumba, Kadar, Hakki Pakki, Jenu Kuruba, Kadu Kuruba, etc.
5. **Western India :** Consisting of Rajasthan, Gujarat and Maharashtra. Some tribes of this area are : Mina, Bhills, Kunbis, Mario Gonds, Mahadev Kolis, Gonds, etc.

3.1.1 Bhills

The Bhills are the one of the largest tribal group in India. The concentration of Bhills in the country is found in four states i.e Gujarat, Maharashtra, Madhya Pradesh and Rajasthan. The districts of Panchmal and Vadodara in Gujarat; Ahmednagar, Aurangabad, Dhule, Jalgoan and Nashik in Maharashtra, Dhar, Jalna, Khargaon and Ratlam in Madhya Pradesh and Banswara, Bhillwara, Chhatisgarh, Kota and Udaypur in Rajasthan are the main residents of the Bhills. According to the census of 1991, the total population of Bhills was about 25 lakhs.

(a) Physical Traits : The world 'Bhilll' comes from the word 'Bhill' which means 'bow' in the Dravidian language. Bhills are well built, strong but short heighted. They are black coloured and broad nose and long hairs.

(b) Habitat : The Bhills mainly live in the hilly areas of Aravali, Vindhaya and Satpura mountains. The climate of this area is monsoon type. The maximum temperature in the month of June is 35°C, while the minimum is 18°C in the month of January. Mid June to September is the period of heavy rain resulting from the monsoon of Arabian Sea.

(c) Settlement : Bhill settlement consists a group of dispersed huts. Cotton cloth is also used to set a tent like house known as *'Pal'*. The huts are half circular in shape. *Pals* are temporary tents. The Bhills built their houses from locally available grass, mud, bamboo or stone. The roofs of the houses are usually built by tiles, though the poor use straw and leaves. The front walls of the huts are generally decorated with painting of lime and red ochre. The house has only a closing door and there is no window. Head of the village is known as 'Vasa'. He and his wife are the honourable persons in the settlement and he also settles the disputes among the inhabitants.

(d) Food and Cloth : Maize is the staple food of the Bhills throughout the year. The small millets like *Kodra, Koori* and *bathi* are also used as a food-grain. Rice is taken on festival and feasts occasions. On the days of festivals such as Rakhi, Diwali and Holi, sweet-rice is principal item. At the time of marriage, rice and boiled grams are also served. Pulses of gram, urad, moong and vegetables are used when available. The Bhills also eat flesh of hare, dear or other animals and birds. On ceremonial occasions they take goats, sheep and buffaloes meat. During rainy season they also take some fishes. The Bhills are much addicted to liquor which is prepared from the flowers of *Mohua* or from the bark of babul or molasses.

Clothing of Bhills differ from region to region. However, the clothing mainly consists of dhoti or longoti and short shirts. The men ordinarily covered their head with a 'turban' which is white coloured. Ladies wear 'ghagra-choli' with a long hand of cloth or '*odhani*'. In Gujarat the Bhills wear *dhoti* which is called '*Potiawal*'. Khandeshi and Madhya Pradesh Bhills wear '*Langoti*'.

Both male and female Bhills wear ornaments made from aurum and bismuth. Ladies wear some specific ornaments as *goth, wale* and metal garlands.

(e) Economy and Occupations : The natural environment of hilly, forested and plateau areas influenced totally the economical pattern of the Bhill. The following are the main occupations of the Bhills :

(i) Agriculture : In Gujarat, subsistence agriculture is mainly performed where they produce jowar, bajra, maize, pulses, *mora, kodo* and *bunti.* Farming practices are very primitive.

(ii) Food Gathering : Bhills of Madhya Pradesh and Satpura range practice food gathering. They collect grass, gum, honey and wild fruits. In the forest they cut wood, collect it into bundles and sell it in the country side. In Madhya Pradesh Bhills collect *Mohua* flowers which are used to prepare local liquor. It is an important business of Bhills. Besides, these they also collect lac, charoli and wax for sale in the country side.

(iii) Livestock Rearing : Bhills in Vindhya region practice this occupation.

(iv) Hunting : Hunting is one of the primitive occupation of Bhills since old times. The bow and arrows are generally used for their hunting.

(f) Social Structure : The Bhills are organised into a number of patrelineal exogamous groups or clans and they have their own social norms with respect to their clans. The clans are generally named after plants or animals to which the clan members ascribe their origin. The tribe is thus sub-divided into a member of clans, each clan based on a common descent and the members of each clan live for the most part in separate *pals* or villages, and observe the rules of exogamy.

(g) Religion and Culture : Bhills are very religious people. They worship number of Hindu Gods like Ram, Maruti, Kalikamata and Sriganesh. Mahadeo is the chief God of Bhills. They also believe in spirit of the jungle. Gujarat and Khandesi Bhills worship variety of Gods like Vaghdeo, Nagdeo, Mhasoba, Asra, Khandoba, Bahiroba. The Bhills have God and Goddesses for every sphere of life. For example, Nangardeo - Goddess of food-grain, Govaldeo - God of herder, Hirkelyo - God of cultivation etc. Bhills celebrate functions anywhere with glory and cheer.

Marriage system of Bhills :

(i) Bhills have their own social norms with respect to their clans or groups.

(ii) Their system of marriage differs from region to region. Ceremonial function about the fixation of marriage locally known as '*Sakharpuda*', is celebrated in the group. After the ceremony the groom approaches the bride's house and offer some amount of money to his mother-in-law. Acceptance of this money by mother-in-law stamps the fixation of marriage binding. Marriages are generally held in summer seasons.

(iii) As dowry system prevails, parents of groom offer dowry to the bride by money or by some gifts like animal wealth. The groom may marry more than once and may have more than single wife.

(iv) Bhills of Madhya Pradesh observe six methods of marriage system i.e. *Shadi, Watra, Udal or Ashwarai, Gharjamai, Bhagoriya* and *Zagda.* Among them Bhagoriya is more common. This system involves the enchroachment with or without the will of the bride by the groom. Bhagoriya implies taking away the bride without any permission or will of her and live with the bride as married woman. Marriage ceremony is completed in due course of time.

(v) In Khandesh, marriage system differs in the sense that a proposal is put about the bride, *Sakharpuda* ceremony is decided on some good day.

(vi) Marriage day is fully celebrated by singing, dancing and enjoying liquor. There is no hard and fast limit of age for marriage, however, late marriages are socially dishonourable.

Bhills Tribe

(a) Habitations : Bhills are also popularly known as the bow men of Rajasthan. They are the most widely distributed tribal group in India. Bhills are mainly divided into two main groups the central or pure bills and eastern or Rajput Bhills.

(b) Language and Costumes :

- Bhills comprise 39% of Rajasthan's total population and speak Bhilli language which is an Indo Aryan language.
- Bhill women wear traditional saris and the Bhill men wear loose long frock along with pyjama. The peasants wear turbans. Bhills also wear brass ornaments.
- Bhills are tall, well built with the handsome features. They are brave and their national weapon is bow made of bamboo. They now practice agriculture as a source of livelihood.

(c) Culture and Religion :

- Most Bhills worship local deities like Khandoba, Kanhoba, Bahiroba, and Sitalmata. Some of the worship Tiger God called 'vaghdev'. They have no temples of their own.
- They consult Badvas the hereditary sorcerers on all the occasions. They are highly superstitious tribal people. They marry only in their own classes. Their close relationships are tightly based on mutual love and respect. They have rich cultural history and gives much importance to dance and music.
- Ghoomar is the most famous dance among the Bhills. Than Gair is the religious dance drama performed by the men in the month of *Sharavana*. The Bhills make beautiful horses, elephants, tigers, deities out of clay.

(d) Fair and Festivals :

- The Baneshwar fair is the main festival celebrated among the Bhills (in the month of January or February). On this occasion Bhills gather all together set up camps on the banks of the Som and Mahi river. They perform dance around the fire and sing traditional songs. Cultural shows, magic shows, animal shows acrobatic feast are the main attraction of the fair. Holi and

Dusshera are the other major festivals celebrated among the Bhills in India.

(e) Backgrounds :

- The Bhills of Gujurat state rebelled on several occasions during the British colonial era, notably in 1846, 1857-58 and 1868.
- The Bhill at present are classified as a Scheduled Tribe in Andhra Pradesh, Chhattisgarh, Gujarat, Karnataka, Maharashtra,Rajasthan, Madhya Pradesh, and Tripura under the Indian government's reservation programmes.

(f) Dress :

- The traditional dresses of men are *Pagri, Angarkha, Dhoti* and *Gamchha.* Traditionally women wear *Sari* and *Ghagra Choli.*
- Men wear *Kada, Bajuband, Chain, ear rings, Kardhani.* Women wear variety of ornaments including *hansli, ring, Zele-zumke, ear ring, narniyan* (bangle), *nathni* (Nose-jewel) etc.
- Tattooing is traditional custom among them.

(g) Religion :

- Every village has its own local God and families have their *Jatidev, Kuldev* and *Kuldevi (house hold deity). 'Bhati dev' and 'Bhillat dev'* are their serpent-god. '*Baba dev*' is their village god. Karkulia dev is their crop god, *Gopal dev* is their pastoral god, Bag dev is their Lion god, *Bhairav dev* is their dog god. Some of their other gods are *Indel dev, Bada dev, Mahadevel, Tejaji, Lotha mai, Techma, Orka Chichma* and *Kajal dev.*
- They have extreme and staunch faith in superstitious beliefs.

(h) Festivals :

- Rakhi, Navratri, Dashera, Diwali, Holi are the main festivals. They also celebrate some traditional festivals viz. *Akhatij, Navmi, Howan Mata ki Chalavani, Sawan Mata ki jatar, Diwasa, Nawai, Bhagoria, Gal, Gar, Dhobi, Sanja, Indel, Doha etc.* with enthusiasm.
- There are a number of tribal fairs held at different places of districts namely Navratri mela, Bhagoria mela etc. Bhill community of Udaipur celebrate Gauari festival.

(i) Political structure

- Traditional Bhill villages are led by a headman who is called as *gameti.* Gameti has authority and decision-making powers over most local disputes or issues.

3.1.2 Gonds

The Gond is one of the largest Dravidian speaking tribes of central India. They are the most civilized aborigins of the country. Once upon a time Gonds were the kings of the land 'Gondwana'. At present the number of Gonds according to the census of 2001, is about three million. They live in the states of Madhya Pradesh, Chhattisgarh, Maharashtra, Orissa and Andhra Pradesh. In Madhya Pradesh Durg, Raipur, Bastar, Baitul, Chhindwada, Shivani and Indore are the main places of Gonds. Bastar district was the homeland of Gond. There are three major groups of Gond i.e. (i) Maria, (ii) Hill Maria and (iii) Bishon Horn Maria. Besides these Parja, Gadaba, Bhatra, Dhakar and Halba are the others. In Andhra Pradesh, the Gonds occupied the parts of Hyderabad empire as Sansthan. Jagdalpur, Dantwara, Kanker, Dhamtari, Rajnandgaon, Dury, Mahasamundra and Raipur district in Chhattisgarh are the main regions of Gonds. Gonds speak 'Gondi' an unwritten language of Dravidian family. But today some of them speak in Hindi, Marathi, Telegu etc. depending on which is dominant in their area.

(a) Climate : The climate of Gond territory is tropical-rainy type where the monthly temperature in January and July reads around 35°C and 20°C respectively. The annual range of temperature remains around 25°C. The mean annual rainfall varies between 120 cm - 180 cm.

(b) Settlement : The Gond live in small clusters made of hamlets which are built upon a large '*bari*' about one hectare in size. They construct their houses from the earthen bricks baked in sun. Generally, the site of the settlement is selected along the river bank, pond or lake to assure the permanent source of water. The houses, known as '*Ghotuls*' are generally built at the end of the village where the unmarried boys and girls sleep in separate dwelling at night. They receive training in civic duties and in sexual practices.

(c) Food and Clothing : The Gonds eat all kinds of meat, including snakes and ants. They also take fruits, millets and food-grains. They consume a locally made liquor of '*Mohua*' flowers. But, with the growing population and depleting natural resources, the Gonds are undernourished and suffering from malnutrition.

Gonds cover their bodies with cotton clothes. Men wear half *dhoti* and *shirt* mostly white in colour. Female adorn themselves with colourful *saris.* Both men and women use silver jewellary.

(d) Occupation : The main occupation of the Gonds are agriculture, fishing, hunting, collecting forest products and livestocks domestication.

Agriculture is performed by two ways : (i) Shifting Cultivation, (ii) Terraced Cultivation.

Shifting cultivation is a traditional type of agriculture. At the beginning a plot is selected. Then the vegetation is burnt and it is cleared off. Seeds of low order crops like maize, jowar, magli are grown in the plot. After 2 to 3 years the cultivated plot is totally abandoned and new site of plot is searched and selected for cultivation. This type of cultivation is commonly known as '*Jhum*' cultivation. The Gonds use generally hoes and digging sticks more than ploughs for cultivation.

In hill and plateau areas of the Bastar district in Chhattisgarh, Gonds practice terrace type of agriculture. The terraces are bordered by logs of wood in such a manner that the flow of water from higher slopes is arrested in successive lower slopes of fields so far. Small water channels are guided to irrigate the field. This practice has evolved from a long series of trial and error. Rice, maize, wheat, barley, pulses are mainly produced here. Terraced cultivation is locally known as '*Penda Krishi*'.

Fishing is one of the main occupation of the 'Kurukh' Gond tribes. They depend on fishing instead of cultivation and exchange fish and food with other Gonds.

Hunting is the other main occupation of Gonds. The Gonds of hill and forest areas are professional hunters. They use mainly arrows and bows for hunting animals and birds. Their methods are very simple and primitive. The forest dwellers are also the food gatherers. They collect the '*Mohua*' flowers for wine production and they use *tadi, shindi, moho* and *koh* types of liquors. From the interior parts of the forests the Gond men collect gum, resin, roots, fruits, seeds, nuts, berries and sal. From the bamboo sticks they can make some useful domestic tools such as baskets, bags, and other things with traditional skills and techniques.

The Gonds also keep oxen and cattle. Oxen are employed in farming operations. One of the sub-tribe 'Rawat Gond' is popular animal herder group of the Gonds. Animal products such as milk, ghee, cheese, meat are obtained from the cattle, sheeps and goats. The animal products are exchanged with the food-grains and domestic materials. Therefore, animal rearing plays an important source of the economy of Gonds since ancient times.

Besides agriculture and animal rearing, there are some household occupations within the clans. Blacksmith plays important role in village economy. Blacksmith prepares agricultural implements such as plough and spears and also many hunting tools.

(e) Social and Cultural Characteristics :

The Gonds are the most advanced and civilized aboriginal tribes of Indian sub-continent. At present though they are classed as tribes, once upon a time they were the rulers of the country known as 'Gondwana'. They are socially well organised but culturally divisible into sub-tribes based on rituals, traditions and occupation. They are culturally most conservative, prefer to remain away from the outer world. Life is wine and music for them. The older and experienced personalities lead all social and cultural functions, decisions and justice. Their marriage matters bear unique rituals and cultural bindings.

Gonds believe in god, spirits and ghosts. The Gonds have shrines in their houses to the spirit of dead ancestors, to the Cobra-God and the sun as well as to the numerous guardian spirits. The tribal Gods are worshipped at an open space near each village. The Gonds sprinkle the blood of victimized animals on seeds. It is believed that such act pleases the Goddesses and harvest blossoms good. Victimization of animals is celebrated with dancing and singing throughout the night.

Habitat

- The Gonds are mostly found in the Gond forests of central India. They are widely found in the Chhindwara District of Madhya Pradesh, Bastar district of Chhattisgarh and also in the parts of Maharashtra, Andhra Pradesh, and Orissa. Gonds call themselves is *Koi* or *Koitur*. Gonds are one of the largest tribal group in the world.

(a) Background :

- Gonds settled in the Gondawa in the ninth and thirteenth century AD. In the fourteen century they ruled several parts of the central India. They built number of forts, palaces, temples, tanks and lakes. The Gondwana kingdom survived till late 16th century. Gond dynasties ruled in four kingdoms - Garha-Mandla, Deogarh, Chanda, and Kherla in the central India. During the British regime in India, Gonds challenged the regime in several battles. They also gained control over the Malwa after the decline of the Mughals followed by the Marathas (1690).

(b) Language :

- Gonds speak Gondi language which is related to the Telegu and the other Dravidian languages. In the northern parts Gonds are often seen speaking the local Hindi and Marathi including Parsi. Gonds are mainly divided into four tribes namely - Raj Gonds, Madia Gonds, Dhurve Gonds, Khatulwar Gonds.
- Gonds men wear *Dhoti.* Women wear soft cotton *saris.* The staple food of Gonds are the two millets known as Kodo or Kutki.
- Rice is the ceremonial feast of the Gonds, which they prefer eating during the time of festivals. Most of the Gonds are the meat consumers.

(c) Religion :

- Gonds have been practicing the Hindu culture and traditions. Gonds are the worshipers of *Janani* or the mother of creator. They use the title *Thakur.*
- Gonds mainly worship Pharsa Pen, who is worshiped under the form of the nail and sometimes a piece of iron chain. Gods including *Mariaiee* (the Goddess of plague and diseases), and Bhimsen the Hindu God.
- Their also exist great number of deities and spirits in the beliefs of Gonds. They say that the earth, water and air are ruled by the great number of deities. They have priests *(devari)* who perform all the religious formalities on all the occasions.
- Gonds also pay homage to the Gods of household, Gods of fields. Animal sacrifice on the religious occasions is the common practice among the Gonds.

(d) Customs and Festivals :

- Keslapur Jathra is the important festival of the Gonds. In this festival they worship the snake deity called *Nagoba. Gusadi* dance is the most famous dance performed by the Gonds. *Madai* is the another major festival celebrated among the Gonds. It is the festival when Gonds meet their relatives settled in various parts of the country.

Science and religion

- Gonds had their own local terms for the Sun, Moon, constellations and Milky Way. Other than Gonds, the Banjaras and Kolams are also known to have knowledge of astronomy.
- Most Gond people follow folk Hinduism which retained the animist beliefs of nature and ancestor worship.
- Among Gonds there are Ravana worshippers whom they consider to be the 10th *dharmaguru* of their people and the ancestor-king of one of their four lineages. They also worship Kupar Lingo as their supreme deity and their ancestor before Ravana. They are a designated Scheduled Tribe in Andhra Pradesh, parts of Uttar Pradesh, Bihar, Chhattisgarh, Gujarat, Jharkhand, Madhya Pradesh, Maharashtra, Telangana, Odisha and West Bengal by the government.

3.1.3 Nagas

Habitat

- The Naga people are ethnic groups in the north eastern part of India and northwestern Myanmar. They form the majority of population Nagaland and Naga Self-Administered Zone of Myanmar; with substantial populations in Manipur, Arunachal Pradesh and Assam in India
- They speak various languages, unique to each tribe. The Nagas have also developed Nagamese Creole. The Naga tribe is divided into various tribes. Some prominent Naga tribes are Angami, Ao, Chakhesang, Konyak, Lotha, Mao, Poumai, Rong mei, Sumi, Tangkhul, Tangshang, Zeme, etc.
- The term "Naga" is derived from a Burmese language word "Naka", which mean "pierced ears" or "people with pierced ears".

(a) Languages :

- The Naga languages are mainly categorized under the Kuki-Chin-Naga languages or the Sal languages. Naga people speak over 89 different languages and dialects.
- According to Per Grierson's classification system, Naga languages can be grouped into Western, Central and Eastern Naga groups. The Western group includes among others Angami, Chokri, Khezha and Rengma.
- The Central Naga group includes Ao, and Lotha; while Eastern group includes Konyak, Phom, Sangtam, Khiamniungan, Yimchunger and Chang tribes. There are Naga-Bodo group illustrated by Mikir language, and Kuki group of languages illustrated by Sopvama and Luppa languages.
- These mostly belong to the Tibeto-Burman language group of the Sino-Tibetan family of languages.
- In 1967 Nagaland proclaimed English as the official language and it is the medium for education in Nagaland. Nagamese, a creole language form of the Assamese language, is a widely spoken language.

(b) Culture and organization :

- The Nagas are organized by tribes differentiated by language and some traditions. The tribes exhibit differences to a certain degree, particularly in their languages and some practices.
- Almost all these Naga tribes have a similar dress code, eating habits, customs, traditional laws, etc. At present the Naga people number around 4 million in total.
- The men's clothing is distinctive: conical red headgear is decorated with wild-boar canine teeth and white-black hornbill feathers.
- Their weapons are primarily a spear, with the shaft decorated with red-black hair, and the machete (*dah*), with broad blade and long handle.
- However Nagas today have culturally much westernised and traditional dresses are rarely used except during their traditional festivals.

(c) Background :

- In 1828 Britain annexed Assam following the Treaty of Yandabo in 1826. In the 1830s, the British sent expeditionary forces, and in 1845, the succeeded in concluding a non-aggression pact with Naga chiefs. But the Naga repeatedly violated the agreement, continuing to raid in Assam.

- After the 1830s, British attempts to annex the region to India were met with sustained and effective guerrilla resistance from Naga groups, particularly the Angami Naga tribe.
- In 1878 the Angamis mounted raids on British camps. The British responded to crush their resistance. Eventually, the region came under the British.
- During the First World War, two thousand Nagas contributed to the war effort on the European front. In the Second World War, they fought to halt the advance of Japanese forces.

Nagas in Myanmar

- Nagas in Myanmar are basically found in Sagaing Division and Kachin state. The Naga territory in Myanmar is marked by Kabo valley in the south bordering to the Chin state, the Kachin on the north and the Burmese on the east.

(d) Social Life of Nagas :

(i) The Nagas are the most popular tribes in the north-eastern frontier region of India. They live basically in the state of Nagaland.

(ii) The Nagas are generally honest and people of integrity. Every Naga considers himself a fine fellow and resents an insult.

(iii) They are exogamous and do not have intra-clan marriage.

(iv) They are superstitious and care too much for good and ill omens.

(v) The Nagas are generally brave. The 'Changs' and 'Semas' are reputed as the most warlike tribes.

(vi) The Nagas believe in guerrilla attack rather than big open fight.

(vi) They generally attack the enemy from behind and conduct their operation with such swiftness that there is no time left for the defender to recover or reorganize.

(vii) The Naga villages are generally small in size and spatially scattered. Almost all the houses are built on the top of steep hills, cliffs, spurs and steep slopes.

(viii) In each village there is a large communal dormitory for bachelors, which is known as '*morung*'. It is like a club. On the other hand, *morung* is a training centre and a guard house.

(ix) The *morung* is also used for the marriage ceremony. The marriages are done by mutual consent of the boys and girls. During a marriage ceremony, when the parents of bride-groom eat, drink and take rest, the bride-groom goes to the morung and spend the night there.

- The Naga tribes have an egalitarian society. The village is a closely knit unit, consisting of intermarried households of different clans.
- The family is the basic unit of the Naga society. Marriages are usually monogamous and fidelity to the spouse is considered a high virtue.
- The Naga society is basically a patriarchal society. They have a strong warrior tradition that valued the birth of boys. A Naga woman is traditionally expected to be obedient and humble.
- The morung is a self-governing body aiming to protect the village and train men to channel fertility into their community.

(e) Art

- The Naga tribes are expert craftsmen and their huts / houses are made of wood and straw and these are ornately carved and arranged. A common practice among all the tribes is decorating the entrances of their dwellings with the heads of buffaloes.
- The Naga people love colour as is evident in the shawls designed and woven by women, and in the headgear that both sexes design. They use beads jewelry, along with a wide range of materials including glass, shell, stone, teeth or tusk, claws, horns, metal, bone, wood, seeds, hair, and fibre.
- Craftwork includes the making of baskets, weaving of cloth, wood carving, pottery, metalwork, jewellary-making and bead-work.
- Weaving colorful woolen and cotton shawls is a central activity for women of all Naga tribes.
- Some of the known shawls include Tsungkotepsu and Rongsu of the Ao tribe; Sutam, Ethasu, Longpensu of the Lothas; Supong of the Santms, Rongkhim and Tsungrem Khim of the Yimchungers; and the Angami Lohe shawls.
- Naga Jewellary is an equally important part of identity, with the entire tribe wearing bead jewellary.

(f) Folk song and dances

- Folk songs and dances are essential ingredients of the traditional Naga culture. The oral tradition is kept alive through the media of folk tales and songs.
- Folk dances of the tribes are mainly performed in groups in synchronized fashion, by both men and women. War dances are performed mostly by men and are athletic and martial in style. Indigenous musical instruments are bamboo mouth organs, cup violins, bamboo flutes, trumpets, drums and log drums etc.

Economy and occupational characteristics of the Nagas in north-eastern part of India.

'Nagas' are one of the well known tribes of north-eastern frontier region of India. There are about 20 groups among the Nagas. This tribe generally belongs to the Indo-Mongoloid race. There are some marked differences between the northern and southern Nagas. But all of them have a symmetry of form and are known for their muscular strength.

The Nagas live in the mountain regions of north-eastern mountain belts. The entire area of the state of Nagaland is hilly and mountainous. On the other hand, this is a monsoon climatic zone. The hot and humid condition and mild winters provide a conducive environment for the growth and development of temperate, evergreen and tropical evergreen dense forests. The physical environments and climatic conditions fully influenced the economy and occupational patterns of the Nagas.

(a) Economy : The 'Nagas' economy is essentially agrarian in character. They largely depend on the *'Jhum'* or shifting cultivation and on forests products for their sustenance. The bamboo trees also play an important role in *'Nagas'* economy. This is utilized in the construction of houses and even in the cooking utensils. The Nagas also use bamboo for their handicraft work.

(b) Occupation : Agriculture is the main occupation of the Nagas. Most of the Nagas are engaged in agriculture and forestry. Nearly 78 per cent of the work force is directly dependent on agriculture while about 1.5 per cent constitutes as agricultural labourers. Livestock, forestry, fishery, hunting, mining and quarrying combined together provide employment to only 0.5

per cent of the work force. Today, a large portion of their population are also engaged in other secondary sectors. However, the main occupational fields of the Nagas are following :

(i) Agriculture : Agriculture is the main occupation of Nagas and '*Jhum*' or shifting cultivation is a form of agriculture in which soil fertility is maintained by field rather than crop rotation. *Jhum* is widely practiced in Nagaland. It covers about 73 per cent of the total aerable land of the state. Under *Jhum*, land is cultivated on hill side tracts as long as it retains sufficient productivity to support the inhabitants, usually from two to three years. Subsequently, the cultivators shifts his cultivation to a new location and develops new fields, leaving the former to lie fallow long enough to regain fertility. The chief crops grown are paddy, maize, beans, yams, red and white pumpkin and cotton. Poppy is also cultivated in the vicinity of the villages and in between the houses sites within securely fenced areas. The Nagas also keep cattles and pigs which feed on the vegetable wastes and inferior grains. The pigs function as buffer-stock which are used during the periods of scarcity or at the time of festivals and feasts.

The shifting cultivation has been criticized on ecological and socio-economic grounds. Because, the large-scale burning of forests, destruction of natural habitats are the adverse result of shifting cultivation. But, it is not so easy to stop the *Jhum* cultivation. Because, the climate, the physical features of the Nagaland, the food habits of the Naga people, their socio-economic and cultural needs, their self-reliance and desire to live close to nature all have a say in shifting cultivation.

(ii) Hunting and Fishing : Hunting and fishing are the other main occupation of the Naga tribe. For hunting they generally use spear and tomahawk. The 'Sing Phos', the one of the branches of Nagas use cross bow while the Kukis use bow in hunting. Angamis Naga use peller-bow for hunting. With these weapons and the trapping system the Nagas can kill smaller animals, birds and also even sambhar, barking dear and pig.

The usual form a fish trap used to erect a weir across a stream, with openings in two or more places at the entrance to which are placed funnel shaped bamboo tubes. Fish swimming down stream enter these tubes, which being too narrow for them to turn they must remain there until removed by fisherman. Hand drag nets are also used in most of the larger stream.

(iii) Handicrafts : Nagas are highly skilled in cottage handicrafts. They have developed great skill in bamboo work, wood work, blacksmithy and pottery making. Bamboo is found in abundance in Nagaland. As raw material being readily available, the Nagas are expert basket makers. Mats and shields of bamboo are also made. The Blacksmiths prepare dao, sickles, axes and spears. Beautiful wood-carving is also to be found on the houses of the wealthy chiefs. The Naga scarf which is a thing of beauty and durability finds a ready market in Shillong, Guwahati, Kolkata and North-Indian cities. The brass ornaments referred are manufactured at a distinct Naga village west of the river Namhpuk. Indian corn wrapping are used in the manufacture of cigars and brought down by the Naga tribes from distant villages to be bartered for salt, ready cash or other commodities. Among themselves the Nagas chiefly trade in paddy which is exchanged for ornaments and beads. The establishment of forest based small industries may also help in boosting up the tribal economy and ultimately their standard of nutrition and overall standard of living.

3.1.4 Tribes in Maharashtra :

(i) The Nomadic tribes in the State of Maharashtra are mainly found in the hilltops but are spread throughout Maharahstra.

(ii) The major tribes which can be found in Maharashtra are Gond-Madia, Bhill, Koli, Warli, Katkari and Oraon. They move about in caravans from one place to another for search for livelihood.

(iii) They come under the category of scheduled tribes according to government of India.

(iv) They heritage of these tribals groups is unique which can be seen by observing their dress, dialect, practices, rites etc.

(v) They still follow the old traditions where the nature is worshipped in different forms. The animals are also sacrificed when a religious ceremony take place.

(vi) The tribes of Maharashtra had the tradition of wandering around in search of work which has led to lack of education in them.

(vii) They are dependent upon firewood, grass, timber etc. to carry on their day-to-day activities. They are organized into small villages that have a chief head of tribe.

(viii) The main survival option for Gond is hunting, farming, eating the fruits from the grove and by selling the cattle as well.

(ix) The number of nomadic tribes in the state is 313 and there are other 198 tribal groups, which are unnoticed.

(x) The Jat Panchayat governs the society of these tribes and the most important role in their life is played by marriage.

(xi) Cultivation and allied activities are practiced by the tribal people of Maharashtra.

(xii) The most prominent tribal community of Maharashtra is Warlis. The beliefs, customs and culture of this community are unique.

(xiii) The Bhill people were initially expert hunters and reside in the deep forest. Gradually they became farmers.

(xiv) The most notable people in Maharashtra are Kolis who are mostly Hindus. You can also find Christian Kolis.

(xv) Another significant tribal community is Halba. The woodcarving of this tribe is very famous and the major occupation of this tribe include animal husbandry, farming and cultivation.

POINTS TO REMEMBER

- A tribe is a social division in a traditional society consisting of families linked by social, economic, religions or blood ties, with a common culture and dialect.
- Constitution of India has recognized tribal communities in India under schedules of the constitution.
- Ministry of Tribal Affairs is responsible for overall development of the scheduled tribes in India.
- There are 461 tribes in India out of which 424 are considered as the scheduled tribes.
- India can be divided into different zones on the basis of distribution and diversity of the tribal population : (i) North zone, (ii) North Eastern zone, (iii) central zone, (iv) Southern zone, (v) Eastern zone (vi) Western zone.
- Dr. B. S. Guha has divided the country into three tribal zones.
  (i) North and North Eastern zone.
  (ii) Central zone
  (iii) Southern zone

- Bhills belong to the race of Pre Aryans.
- The Gonds are mostly found in the Gond forests of central India.
- The Naga people are ethnic groups in the North eastern part of India and northwestern Myanmar.
- The state of Nagaland was formally recognized on 1st December 1963 as the 16th state of the Indian union.
- The major tribes which can be found in Maharashtra are Gond-Madia, Bhill, Koli, Warli Katkari, Oraon etc.

✧ QUESTIONS ✧

Q. I : Answer the following questions in detail.

(1) *Which are the major tribes in India ?*

(2) *State is the Regional distribution of Tribes in India ?*

(3) *Write about the Bhills with reference to :*
   - (i) *Language and costumes*
   - (ii) *Culture and Religion*
   - (iii) *Festivals*

(4) *Write about the Gonds with special reference to the following*
   - (i) *Background*
   - (ii) *Language*
   - (iii) *Religion*

(5) *Write about Nagas with special reference to :*
   - (i) *Habitat*
   - (ii) *Languages*
   - (iii) *Culture*

(6) *What are the tribes in Maharashtra ? What is their distribution ?*

Q. II : Write short notes :

(1) *Ministry of Tribal Affairs*

(2) *Gonds*

(3) *Bhills*

(4) *Nagas*

(5) *Tribes in Maharashtra*

❋ ❋ ❋

UNIT – 4

HUMAN CULTURE

SYNOPSIS

INTRODUCTION

Language is what people use to communicate with each other. They can do this by speaking, writing, waving their hands or moving their body to show others what they mean. Writing began about 5,000 years ago.

People learn to speak naturally however they must be taught to write. Spoken language comes from sounds that form words and sentences that have a certain meaning. We use language to express our ideas and feelings.

Languages have rules, called grammar. Thousands of languages have evolved globally during history. They all use different sounds and different words. Almost all languages are influenced by other languages and borrow words from them. Written languages use an alphabet to form words and sentences. The Latin alphabet is the popular, used by many languages. Other languages, i.e. Chinese and Arabic use their own writing systems.

There are many religions in the world. The main world religions are : Christianity, Islam, Hinduism, Buddhism, Sikhism, Judaism.

The five oldest world religions are Hinduism, Judaism, Christianity, Buddhism, Islam.

4.1 World Languages and their Distribution

World Language (Meaning) :

A world language is one that is spoken internationally and learned and spoken by numerous people as a second language. A world language is not only characterized by the total number of speakers but also by geographical distribution and its use in international organizations and diplomatic relations.

Table 4.1

Languages	Total Speaker Natives, First and Second Language speakers (in millions)
English	2100
Mandarin Chinese	1100
Spanish	530
Hindi	500
Arabic	350
French	230
Russian	270
Portuguese	217
German	110

- The most widely spoken (and likely the fastest spreading) world language today is English, with over 1.1 billion native and second-language users worldwide. On similar grounds, French and Spanish are also categorized as world languages including Arabic, Mandarin Chinese, Russian and Portuguese.
- Historically, Egyptian, Ancient Greek, Latin, Classical Chinese, Persian, Sanskrit and Classical Arabic have also functioned as world languages due to their previous standings.

(I) Asian languages

(a) Arabic

- Arabic language gained international recognition due to medieval Islamic conquests and Urbanization of the Middle East and North Africa. It is also a language among the Muslim outside the Arab World.

(b) Chinese

- Standard Chinese today serves as a common language between speakers of other varieties of Chinese not only within but also overseas Chinese communities. It is also widely taught as a second language internationally.

(c) Persian

- Persian, (South-Western Iranian language) used to be the language of non-Arabic parts of the Islamic world (Greater Iran, Anatolia and the Indian subcontinent in particular) during the medieval and early modern periods. Persian language also served as the official language of the empires, from the Delhi to Constantinople in the Ottoman Empire.

(d) Indian languages

- The main languages of the Indian subcontinent have numbers of speakers which can be compared to those of major world languages basically due to the large population in the region rather than a supra-regional use of these languages. Hindi, Urdu, Bengali and Tamil may fulfill the criteria in terms of supra-regional usage and international recognition. Tamil is spoken in Southern India. Tamil is an official language in Sri Lanka and Singapore, a minority language in the constitution of South Africa and one of the three recognized languages of education in Malaysia. The native speaking population of Bengali vastly outnumber those who speak French as a first language, and it is one of the most spoken languages (ranking fifth or sixth in the world with nearly 230 million total speakers, and is known for its long and rich literary tradition.

(II) European languages

(a) English

- English language has 370 million native speakers. English is estimated to have over 610 million second-language speakers. English is increasingly becoming the dominant language of scientific research and papers worldwide, having even outpaced national languages. English is the most common of the languages used on the Internet. As of 2019, according to study, English language is used by 54.0% of the world's top 10 million websites and according to another study 25.5% of the Internet users are English speakers.

(b) French

- During the 19th, 20th centuries, French was the language of communication and the favoured second language among the educated classes in Europe, Russia, Romania, Bulgaria, Greece, Syria, Egypt, Ottoman Turkey and Iran.
- French language enjoyed high status in some southeast Asian countries i.e. Vietnam, Laos and Cambodia, and several South American ones like Argentina, Brazil, Chile, and Uruguay.
- However, French has declined steadily, being gradually displaced by English although in Lebanon, Tunisia, Algeria and Morocco, French continues to be the favoured second language, as well as enjoying official status in Canada, Switzerland and Belgium.
- French language still remains one of the working languages of many international organizations, i. e. United Nations, NATO, European Union and NAFTA. French is the principal working language of the European Court of Justice.

(c) German

- German served as the language in large portions of Europe for centuries, (Holy Roman Empire and later the Austro-Hungarian Empire). It is an important second language in much of Central and Eastern Europe, and in the international scientific community.

- It is the most spoken native language in the European Union. As of 2019, it is the third most commonly used language for website content, with 5.8% of the world's top 10 million websites using it, and 2.1% of all Internet users are German speakers.

(d) Russian

- Russian is the largest language in Europe, the most widespread language in Eurasia, one of the six official languages of the United Nations, and one of two official languages aboard the International Space Station.
- As present it is the second most used language for website content, with 5.9% of the world's top 10 million websites using it, and 2.5% of all Internet users are Russian speakers.
- Russian language was used in the Russian Empire and the Soviet Union, and its teaching was compulsory in the Eastern Bloc countries.
- However, the use of Russian language has reduced in both the former Eastern bloc and abroad since the break up of the Soviet Union, Russian language is still widely spoken throughout the Caucasus, Central Asia, Eastern Europe and the Baltic states.

(e) Spanish

- Spanish is the world's second-most spoken native language after Mandarin Chinese. Spanish is used in the Spanish Empire and today is in use in Spain, in Latin American countries and is widely spoken in many parts of the U.S. particularly in Florida and the states which border Mexico.
- Spanish became the most widely taught non-English language in American secondary schools and schools of higher education. It is also an official language of the United Nations.
- In 2019, Spanish had the third largest number of internet users by language with 7.9%, after English with 25.2% and Chinese with 19.3%.

(f) Historical Languages :

- Historical languages include Egyptian in Ancient Egypt, Sumerian, Akkadian and Aramaic in the various Mesopotamian civilizations; Ancient Greek in the Greek colonies evolving to Koine Greek in the Hellenistic world, and subsequently in the eastern part of the Roman Empire and the territories of the Byzantine Empire; Latin in the Roman Empire and presently as the standard liturgical language for the Catholics Classical Chinese in East Asia during the Imperial era of Chinese history; Persian during the various succeeding Persian Empires, and once served as the second language of the Islamic World after Arabic; Sanskrit during the ancient and medieval historical periods of various states in South Asia, Southeast Asia, and Central Asia.
- The Roman languages is an evidence of Latin as the lingua franca of the Roman. Italian language nowadays is the most-spoken language among members of the Roman Catholic hierarchy, and it is also used in music (especially Opera) and the fashion industry.
- Turkish was similarly important as the primary language of the Ottoman Empire.
- A number of international auxiliary languages have been introduced as prospective world languages, the most successful of them being Esperanto.

4.1.1 Current Distribution of Human Language Families

- All rankings should be used with precaution, because it is not possible to devise a coherent set of linguistic criteria for distinguishing languages. For example, a language is often defined as a set of varieties that are mutually intelligible, but independent national standard languages may be considered to be separate languages even though they are largely mutually intelligible i.e. Danish and Norwegian language.
- Conversely, many commonly accepted languages, including German, Italian and even English, encompass varieties that are not mutually intelligible.

- There are difficulties in getting reliable data about speakers, which differ over time because of population change and language shift.

Top languages by population

- The following languages are listed as having at least 10 million first language speakers in the 2019 edition of Ethnologue, (published by SIL International).

Table 4.2

Rank	Language	Speakers (Millions)	% of the World population	Language family Branch
1	Mandarin Chinese	918	11.922	Sino-Tibetan Sinitic
2	Spanish	480	5.994	Indo-European Romance
3	English	379	4.922	Indo-European Germanic
4	Hindi (Sanskritised Hindustani)	341	4.429	Indo-European Indo-Aryan
5	Bengali	228	2.961	Indo-European Indo-Aryan
6	Portuguese	221	2.870	Indo-European Romance
7	Russian	154	2.000	Indo-European Balto-Slavic
8	Japanese	128	1.662	Japonic Japanese
9	Western Punjabi	92.7	1.204	Indo-European Indo-Aryan
10	Marathi	83.1	1.079	Indo-European Indo-Aryan
11	Telugu	82.0	1.065	Dravidian South-Central
12	Wu Chinese	81.4	1.057	Sino-Tibetan Sinitic
13	Turkish	79.4	1.031	Turkic Oghuz

Contd.

14	Korean	77.3	1.004	Koreanic language isolate
15	French	77.2	1.003	Indo-European Romance
16	German	76.1	0.988	Indo-European Germanic
17	Vietnamese	76.0	0.987	Austroasiatic Vietic
18	Tamil	75.0	0.974	Dravidian South
19	Yue Chinese	73.1	0.949	Sino-Tibetan Sinitic
20	Urdu (Persianised Hindustani)	68.6	0.891	Indo-European Indo-Aryan
21	Javanese	68.3	0.887	Austronesian Malayo-Polynesian
22	Italian	64.8	0.842	Indo-European Romance
23	Egyptian Arabic	64.6	0.839	Afroasiatic Semitic
24	Gujarati	56.4	0.732	Indo-European Indo-Aryan
25	Iranian Persian	52.8	0.686	Indo-European Iranian
26	Bhojpuri	52.2	0.678	Indo-European Indo-Aryan
27	Min Nan Chinese	50.1	0.651	Sino-Tibetan Sinitic
28	Hakka Chinese	48.2	0.626	Sino-Tibetan Sinitic
29	Jin Chinese	46.9	0.609	Sino-Tibetan Sinitic
30	Hausa	43.9	0.570	Afroasiatic Chadic
31	Kannada	43.6	0.566	Dravidian South
32	Indonesian (Indo nesian Malay)	43.4	0.564	Austronesian Malayo-Polynesian

Contd.

33	Polish	39.7	0.516	Indo-European Balto-Slavic
34	Yoruba	37.8	0.491	Niger–Congo Volta–Niger
35	Xiang Chinese	37.3	0.484	Sino-Tibetan Sinitic
36	Malayalam	37.1	0.482	Dravidian South
37	Odia	34.5	0.448	Indo-European Indo-Aryan
38	Maithili	33.9	0.440	Indo-European Indo-Aryan
39	Burmese	32.9	0.427	Sino-Tibetan Lolo-Burmese
40	Eastern Punjabi	32.6	0.423	Indo-European Indo-Aryan
41	Sunda	32.4	0.421	Austronesian Malayo-Polynesian
42	Sudanese Arabic	31.9	0.414	Afroasiatic Semitic
43	Algerian Arabic	29.4	0.382	Afroasiatic Semitic
44	Moroccan Arabic	27.5	0.357	Afroasiatic Semitic
45	Ukrainian	27.3	0.355	Indo-European Balto-Slavic
46	Igbo	27.0	0.351	Niger–Congo Volta–Niger
47	Northern Uzbek	25.1	0.326	Turkic Karluk
48	Sindhi	24.6	0.319	Indo-European Indo-Aryan
49	North Levantine Arabic	24.6	0.319	Afroasiatic Semitic
50	Romanian	24.3	0.316	Indo-European Romance
51	Tagalog	23.6	0.306	Austronesian Malayo-Polynesian

Contd.

52	Dutch	23.1	0.300	Indo-European Germanic
53	Sa'idi Arabic	22.4	0.291	Afroasiatic Semitic
54	Gan Chinese	22.1	0.287	Sino-Tibetan Sinitic
55	Amharic	21.9	0.284	Afroasiatic Semitic
56	Northern Pashto	20.9	0.271	Indo-European Iranian
57	Magahi	20.7	0.269	Indo-European Indo-Aryan
58	Thai	20.7	0.269	Kra–Dai Tai
59	Saraiki	20.0	0.260	Indo-European Indo-Aryan
60	Khmer	16.6	0.216	Austroasiatic Khmer
61	Chhattisgarhi	16.3	0.212	Indo-European Indo-Aryan
62	Somali	16.2	0.210	Afroasiatic Cushitic
63	Malay (Malaysian Malay)	16.1	0.209	Austronesian Malayo-Polynesian
64	Cebuano	15.9	0.206	Austronesian Malayo-Polynesian
65	Nepali	15.8	0.205	Indo-European Indo-Aryan
66	Mesopotamian Arabic	15.7	0.204	Afroasiatic Semitic
67	Assamese	15.3	0.199	Indo-European Indo-Aryan
68	Sinhala	15.3	0.199	Indo-European Indo-Aryan
69	Northern Kurdish	14.6	0.190	Indo-European Iranian
70	Hejazi Arabic	14.5	0.188	Afroasiatic Semitic

Contd.

71	Nigerian Fulfulde	14.5	0.188	Niger–Congo Senegambian
72	Bavarian	14.1	0.183	Indo-European Germanic
73	South Azerbaijani	13.8	0.179	Turkic Oghuz
74	Greek	13.1	0.170	Indo-European Hellenic
75	Chittagonian	13.0	0.169	Indo-European Indo-Aryan
76	Kazakh	12.9	0.168	Turkic Kipchak
77	Deccan	12.8	0.166	Indo-European Indo-Aryan
78	Hungarian	12.6	0.164	Uralic Ugric
79	Kinyarwanda	12.1	0.157	Niger–Congo Bantu
80	Zulu	12.1	0.157	Niger–Congo Bantu
81	South Levantine Arabic	11.6	0.151	Afroasiatic Semitic
82	Tunisian Arabic	11.6	0.151	Afroasiatic Semitic
83	Sanaani Spoken Arabic	11.4	0.148	Afroasiatic Semitic
84	Min Bei Chinese	11.0	0.143	Sino-Tibetan Sinitic
85	Southern Pashto	10.9	0.142	Indo-European Iranian
86	Rundi	10.8	0.140	Niger–Congo Bantu
87	Czech	10.7	0.139	Indo-European Balto-Slavic
88	Ta'izzi-Adeni Arabic	10.5	0.136	Afroasiatic Semitic

Contd.

89	Uyghur	10.4	0.135	Turkic Karluk
90	Min Dong Chinese	10.3	0.134	Sino-Tibetan Sinitic
91	Sylheti	10.3	0.134	Indo-European Indo-Aryan

Source : Wikipedia

Major language families in the world.

- Language is a system of conventional spoken or written symbols by which human-beings can communicate with each other.
- Language can be classified precisely on the basis of origin and development which is called as genetic classification. There are major principal linguistic families or groups in the world and they are as follows :

(I) The Indo-European Language Family : This linguistic family is the largest of all in the world. It is dominant in Europe, Russia, North and South America, Australia and parts of South-Western Asia and India.

- The first speakers of this language were Kurgans, who lived in the Steppes to the North of Caspian Sea near the Volga River about 5000 years ago. Between 3500 and 2500 B. C., the Kurgans migrated to the west through Europe, Eastern Siberia and South-East to South Asia.
- In later period as they lost contact with one another, different Indo-European groups developed various forms of language. There are eight branches of Indo-European language. They are as follows :
  (a) Germanic - German, English, Scandinavian.
  (b) Romance - French, Italian, Spanish.
  (c) Balto-slavic, Russian. (d) Indo-Iranian.
  (e) Greek. (f) Celtic.
  (g) American. (h) Alabanian.

(a) Germanic Family : The Germanic language has three branches i.e. North Germanic, East Germanic and West Germanic. The North Germanic includes the Scandinavian language. The East Germanic language was known as Gothic. Today, it has no existence as the Gothic tribe were converted to other languages through political dominance. West Germanic includes German, Anglo Saxon, English, Dutch and Flemish languages. In this group, English is an important language which was originated mainly from German, spread all over the world with the compass of British empire.

(b) Romance Family : The Romance Family is also known as 'The Latin linguistic family'. French, Italian, Spanish, Portuguese and Romanian are the main languages of this group. Like English, the Latin languages, especially Spanish and Portugese have achieved world wide prominence because of the colonial activities of their speakers.

- French is the language of France and it has been adopted as a national language in Switzerland, Canada and several countries of Africa. Italian language has its major concentration in Italy, Sicily, Switzerland and some islands in the Mediterranean Sea, while Romania is the official language of Romania.

(c) Balto-slavic Language : This type of language is divided into East and South languages. The most widely used Eastern Slavic language is Russian. The other two Balto-slavic languages are Ukrainian and Byelorussian. The West Slavic languages include Polish, Czech and Slavic Bulgarian, Serbo Croatian, Slovene and Macedonian belong to the South Slavic languages group.

(d) Indo-Iranian Languages : The Indo - Iranian language family include more than one hundred individual languages. The people of Bangladesh, Pakistan, India and Western part of Iran use these languages.

- In Pakistan, Urdu is a principal language, while Hindi is national language of India. The people of Bangladesh and West Bengal of India speak Bengali.

(i) Sino-Tibetan Languages Family : The Sino-Tibetan linguistic family is dominated mainly by Chinese, Many smaller countries of South-East Asia also use this language. More than 500 million people speak Sino-Tibetan language.

- The most important language of China is Mandarin, which is spoken by three fourth of the total population of China. Other Sino-Tibetan languages consist Thai, Tibetan and Burmese or Myanmari. Japanese and Korean are the other important languages which are related to Chinese by origin.

(ii) Semito-Hametic Languages Family : This group of languages cover the area from Arabian Peninsular and the Tigris-Euphrates river valley of Iraq westward through Syria and North Africa to the Atlantic Ocean. It originated during pre-historic times. Ancient Babylonians, Assyrians and Phoenecians used this language.

- The most widespread sematic language is Arabic. Hebrew is spoken by three million people mainly in Israel. When Israel was formed in 1948, Hebrew became less useful language. People of North and East Africa speak Hametic language though these number is quite small.

(iii) African Languages Family : There is no definite language in Africa. Nearly 1000 distinct languages as well as several thousand named dialects have been accounted in Africa. In Northern part of this continent Arabia is widely used.

- In the South of Sahara the main language is 'Negro-Congo' which has six branches viz. Mande Crur, Kwa, Adamawa and Benue-Congo. In Northern part of 'Nigro-Congo' 'Nilo-Saharan' languages are used. The Kholsan language family is found in South Western Africa. Hausa and other 200 languages are used in Nigeria. Swahili is the official language of Tanzania and East African countries.

(iv) Other languages : Malya - Polynesian is one of the remarkable language family in the world which is spoken by the people of Madagascar to Indonesia, and Pacific Islands to Hawaii.

- Ural-Altaic is and another language. The speakers of this language are found in cold deserts, Taiga lands of Eurasia as far West as Turkey, Hungary and Finland.
- The Dravidian languages are spoken mainly by South Indian people. Amerindian, Eskimoan, Cauccasian etc. are some native languages have been spotted here and there.

4.2 World Major Religions and their Distribution

4.2.1 Major religious groups

- In the 18th century, **Freidrich Schleirmacher** defined, "*religion as feeling of absolute dependence.*"

  William Jones called, "*religion as 'the enthusiastic temper of exposal*".

  Otto defines, "*the essence of religious awareness as awe, a unique blend of fear and fascination before the divine. Religion is a symbol of group identity and cultural rallying point.*"
- Sociologist Durkheim said that "religion is a system of beliefs and rituals with reference to the sacred which bind people together into social groups."

Major Religious Groups : There are about 5 religions in the world. Out of these following are the main religions.

- The world's principal religions may be classified into a small number of major groups, although this is by no means a uniform practice.

History of Religious Categories :

- In world cultures, there have traditionally been many different groupings of religious belief.
- **Daniel Defoe** described the original definition of religion as follows: "*Religion is properly the Worship given to God, but it is also applied to the Worship of Idols and false Deities.*"
- In 1838, the four-way division of Christianity, Judaism, Mahommedanism and Paganism was done by Josiah Conder includes Druze, Yezidis, Mandeans, and Elamites under a list of possibly monotheistic groups, and under "polytheism and pantheism," he listed Zoroastrianism, "Vedas, Puranas,

Tantras, Reformed sects" of India as well as "Brahminical idolatry," Buddhism, Jainism, Lamaism, "religion of China and Japan," and "illiterate superstitions" as others. The modern meaning of "world religion," putting non-Christians at the same level as Christians, began with the 1893 Parliament of the World's Religions in Chicago. During the latter half of the 20th century, the category of "world religion" fell into serious question. Abrahamic religions originate in West Asia, Indian religions in the Indian subcontinent (South Asia) and East Asian religions in East Asia. Another group with supra-regional influence are Afro-American religion, which have originated in Central and West Africa.

Middle Eastern religions

- Abrahamic religions are the largest group, of religions consisting mainly of Judaism, Christianity, Islam, and the Bahá'í Faith. Today, at least 3.8 billion people are followers of Abrahamic religions and are spread widely around the world apart from the regions around East and Southeast Asia.
- Iranian religions, partly of Indo-European origins, include Zoroastrianism, Yazdânism, Uatsdin, Yarsanism and historical traditions of Gnosticism (Mandaeism, Manichaeism).
- Indian religions, originated in Greater India and consist of dharma, karma, reincarnation among others. They are of the most influence across the Indian subcontinent, East Asia, Southeast Asia, as well as isolated parts of Russia. The main Indian religions are Hinduism, Jainism, Buddhism and Sikhism.
- East Asian religions consist of several East Asian religions which include many Chinese folk religions, Taoism and Confucianism, as well as Korean and Japanese religion.

African religions

- The religions of the tribal peoples of Sub-Saharan Africa, but excludes ancient Egyptian religion, which is considered to belong to the ancient Middle East.

- African diasporic religions practiced in the Americas, imported as a result of the Atlantic slave trade of the 16th to 18th centuries. Indigenous ethnic religions, found on every continent, getting sidelined by the major organized religions in many parts of the world. Includes traditional African religions, Asian shamanism, Native American religions, Austronesian and Australian Aboriginal traditions, Chinese folk religions and postwar Shinto.
- New religious movement is the term applied to any religious faith which has emerged since the 19th century, often syncretizing, re-interpreting or reviving aspects of older traditions such as Ayyavazhi, Mormonism, Ahmadiyya, Pentecostalism, Polytheistic reconstructionism etc.

Religious demographics

- One way to define a major religion is by the number of current followers. The population numbers by religion are computed by a combination of census reports and population surveys.
- There is no agreement among researchers as to the best methodology for determining the religiosity profile of the world's population.

Table 4.3. : Largest religious groups

Religion	Number of followers (in billions)	Cultural tradition	Founded
Christianity	2.4	Abrahamic religions	Middle East
Islam	1.9	Abrahamic religions	Middle East
Hinduism	1.1	Indian religions	Indian subcontinent
Buddhism	0.52	Indian religions	Indian subcontinent
Folk religion	0.4	Depends on the region	All around globe

Table 4.4 : Medium-sized religions

The following are medium-sized world religions:

Religion	Number of followers (in millions)	Cultural tradition
Taoism	12–173	Chinese religions
Shinto	100	Japanese religions
Falun Gong	80–100	Chinese religions
Sikhism	30	Indian religions
Judaism	14.5	Abrahamic religions
Confucianism	6–7	Chinese religions
Spiritism	5-15	New religious movements
Korean shamanism	5–15	Korean religions
Caodaism	5–9	Vietnamese religions
Bahá'í Faith	5–7.3	Abrahamic religions
Tenriism	5	Japanese religions
Jainism	4	Indian religions
Cheondoism	3–4	Korean religions
Hoahaoism	1.5–3	Vietnamese religions

Table 4.5 : List of religious populations

Religion	Percent
Christianity	31.5%
Islam	23.2%
Unaffiliated	16.3%
Hinduism	15%
Buddhism	7.1%
Folk Religion	5.9%
Other (includes Judaism, Bahá'í, Sikhism, and Jainism)	1.0%

Pew Research Centre, 2012. This is a list of religious populations by number of adherents and countries.

Table 4. 6 : Adherent estimates in 2019

Religion	Adherents	Percentage
Christianity	2.4 billion	29.81%
Islam	1.9 billion	23.60%
Secular/Non religious /Agnostic /Atheist	1.2 billion	14.91%
Hinduism	1.15 billion	14.28%
Buddhism	521 million	6.47%
Chinese traditional religion[c]	394 million	4.89%
Ethnic religions excluding some in separate categories	300 million	3.37%
African traditional religions	100 million	1.24%
Sikhism	30 million	0.37%
Spiritism	15 million	0.19%
Judaism	14.5 million	0.18%
Bahá'í	7.0 million	0.09%
Jainism	4.2 million	0.05%
Shinto	4.0 million	0.05%
Cao Dai	4.0 million	0.05%
Zoroastrianism	2.6 million	0.03%
Tenrikyo	2.0 million	0.02%
Neo-Paganism	1.0 million	0.01%
Unitarian Universalism	0.8 million	0.01%
Rastafari	0.6 million	0.01%
Total	**8.0507 billion**	**100%**

Christians

Countries with the greatest proportion of Christians from Christianity by country (as of 2010)

Christian population by country, June 2014.

Vatican City 100% (100% Roman Catholic), Pitcairn Islands 100% (100% Seventh-day Adventist), Samoa ~ 99% (mostly Protestant) , Romania 99% (mostly Romanian Orthodox), American

Samoa 98.3% (mostly Protestant), Malta 98.1% (mostly Roman Catholic), Venezuela 98% (71% Roman Catholic), Greece 98% (95% Greek Orthodox), Marshall Islands 97.2% (mostly Protestant), Tonga 97.2% (mostly Protestant), San Marino 97% (~97% Roman Catholic), Paraguay 96.9% (mostly Roman Catholic), Peru 96.5% (mostly Roman Catholic), El Salvador 96.4% (mostly Roman Catholic), Kiribati 96% (mostly Protestant), Federated States of Micronesia ~96% (mostly Protestant), Barbados 95.1% (mostly Protestant), Papua New Guinea 94.8% (mostly Protestant), East Timor 94.2% (mostly Roman Catholic), Armenia 93.5% (mostly Armenian Orthodox)

Muslims

Countries with the greatest proportion of Muslims from Islam country.

Muslim population by country, 2014.

Afghanistan 99.7% (mostly Sunni, 20% Shi'a), Tunisia 99.5% (mostly Sunni), Iran 99.4% (mostly Shi'a), Azerbaijan 99.2% (65-75% Shi'a), Yemen 99.1% (35-40% Shi'a), Mauritania 99.1%, Morocco ~99%, Iraq 99% (65-70% Shi'a), Niger 98.6% (mostly Sunni), Somalia 98.5% (mostly Sunni), Maldives 98.4% (mostly Sunni) Comoros 98.3% (mostly Sunni), Algeria 98%, Turkey ~98%, Saudi Arabia ~97% (10-15% Shi'a), Djibouti 96.9% (mostly Sunni) , Libya 96.6% (Mostly Sunni), Pakistan 96.4%, Kuwait ~95% (20-25% Shi'a), Egypt 94.6% (Mostly Sunni), Bangladesh 89.6% (Mostly Sunni), Indonesia 88.2% (Mostly Sunni), Bahrain 81.2% (65-75% Shi'a) (Mostly Shi'a), Sierra Leone 78.00% (mostly Sunni)], Sudan 71.3% (mostly Sunni), Malaysia 60.4% (mostly Sunni),

Irreligious and atheist : Non-religious population by country, 2007. Countries with the greatest proportion of people without religion. Estonia 71–82% (77%), Czech Republic 70-81% (76%), Japan 64–88% (76%), Denmark 72%, Sweden 46–82% (64%), Vietnam 44–81% (63%), Macau 62%, Hong Kong 57%, France 43–64% (54%), Norway 31–72% (52%), China 47% (details), Netherlands 39–55% (47%), Finland 28–60% (44%), New Zealand 42%, United Kingdom 31–52% (42%), England and Wales 25%,

South Korea 30–52% (41%), Germany 25–55% (40%), Hungary 32–46% (39%), Belgium 42–43% (39%), Bulgaria 34–40% (37%), Slovenia 35–38% (37%), Russia 13–48% (31%).

Irreligious includes agnostic, atheist, secular believer, and people having no formal religious adherence. It does not necessarily mean that members of this group don't belong to any religion.

Hindus

Countries with the greatest proportion of Hindus from Hinduism by country 2013 :

Nepal 81.3%, India 79.8%, Mauritius 48.54%, Fiji 27.9%, Bhutan 25%, Guyana 24.8%, Suriname 22.3%, Trinidad and Tobago 18.2%, United Arab Emirates 15%, Sri Lanka 12.6%, Kuwait 12%, Bangladesh 9.6%, Bahrain 8.1%, Réunion 6.7%, Malaysia 6.3%, Singapore 5.1%, Oman 3%, Seychelles 2.1%, New Zealand 2.0%, Pakistan 1.8%, Indonesia 1.7%, United Kingdom 1.7%, United States 0.7%.

Buddhists

Countries with the greatest proportion of Buddhists from Buddhism by country (as of 2010) :

Cambodia 96.9%, Thailand 93.2%, Myanmar 80.1%, Laos 66.0%, Bhutan 74.70%, Sri Lanka 69.3%, Mongolia 55.1%, Japan 36.2%, Taiwan 35.1%, Singapore 33.2%, South Korea 22.9%, Malaysia 19.8 %, China 18.2%, Macau 17.3%, Vietnam 16.4%, Hong Kong 13.2%, Nepal 10.3%

Taoists/Confucianists/Chinese traditional religionists

As a spiritual practice, Taoism has made fewer inroads in the West than Buddhism and Hinduism. Taiwan 33–80%, China 30%, Hong Kong 28%, Macau 13.9%, Singapore 8.5%, Malaysia 2.6%, South Korea 0.2–1%, Vietnam, Philippines 0.01–0.05%, Indonesia 0.05%.

The Chinese traditional religion has 184,000 believers in Latin America, 250,000 believers in Europe, and 839,000 believers in North America as of 1998.

Ethnic and indigenous

All of the below come from the U.S. Department of State 2009 International Religious Freedom Report.

Haiti 50%, Guinea-Bissau 50%, Cameroon 40%, Togo 33%, Côte d'Ivoire 25%, Sudan 25%, Benin 23%, Burundi 20%, Burkina Faso 15%, New Zealand 15%, South Africa 15%, Democratic Republic of the Congo 12% ,Central African Republic 10%, Gabon 10%, Lesotho 10%, Nigeria 10%, Sierra Leone 10%, Indonesia 9%, Kenya 9%, Palau 9%, Ghana 8.5%, Guinea 5%.

Sikhism

Countries with the greatest proportion of Sikhs:

India 1.9%, United Kingdom 1.2%, Canada 0.9%, Malaysia 0.5%, Singapore 0.3%, United States 0.2%, Fiji 0.3%, New Zealand 0.2%, Australia 0.1%, Italy 0.1%.

The Sikh homeland is the Punjab state, in India, where today Sikhs make up approximately 61% of the population. This is the only place where Sikhs are in the majority.

Spiritism

Cuba 10.3%, Jamaica 10.2%,Brazil 4.8% Suriname 3.6%, Haiti 2.7% Dominican Republic 2.2%, The Bahamas 1.9% Nicaragua 1.5% Trinidad and Tobago 1.4%, Guyana 1.3%, Venezuela 1.1%, Colombia 1.0%, Belize 1.0%, Honduras 0.9%, Puerto Rico 0.7%, Panama 0.5%, Iceland 0.5%, Guadeloupe 0.4%, Argentina 0.2%, Guatemala 0.2%.

Judaism

Countries with the greatest proportion of Jews (as of 2017) : Israel 73.6%, Gibraltar 2.0%, United States 1.76%, Canada 1.07%, France 0.7%, Hungary 0.485%, Uruguay 0.483%, Australia 0.47%, Latvia 0.24%, U.S. Virgin Islands 0.36%, United Kingdom 0.44%, Argentina 0.41%, Bermuda 0.154%,Panama 0.250%, Belgium 0.259 %, Switzerland 0.22%,South Africa 0.124%, Panama 0.250%, Netherlands 0.17%, NewZealand0.16%, Estonia 0.154%, Sweden 0.1 52%,Germany 0.1%Ukraine 0.124%, Russia 0.122%, Denmark 112%.

Bahá'ís

Countries with the greatest proportion of Bahá'ís (as of 2010) with a national population ≥200,000:

Belize 2.5% Bolivia 2.2%, Zambia 1.8%, Mauritius 1.8%,Vanuatu 1.4%, Barbados 1.2%, Trinidad and Tobago 1.2%, Panama 1.2%, Kenya 1.0% Lesotho 0.9%, Papua NewGuinea 0.9%, Réunion 0.9 % Chad 0.9%, Botswana 0.8%, Gambia 0.8%, Suriname 0.8% , Congo, Republic of the 0.6%, Solomon Islands 0.6%, Venezuela 0.6%.

Jainism

India 0.3%, Suriname 0.3%, Fiji 0.2%, Kenya 0.2, Nepal 0.1%.

Geographers generally classify religion as follows :

Major Religious Groups : There are about 5 religions in the world. Out of these following are the main religions.

(A) Christianity : Christianity is so far the largest religion both in area and in number of believers. According to an estimate in 2015, the total population of Christians is about 2.4 billion. Early beginners carried it to Greek lands and then it spread to many other parts of the world. Christianity emerged from ethnic religion Judaism as a reform activity.

- The Christian faith spread across a large part of the earth into several million people, converts and overtook many cultural groups in the world. Initially there were Eastern and Western Christian thoughts in Europe. Eastern group was highly orthodox in Greek and Slavic lands of Eastern and Southern Europe.
- There are two branches of Eastern Christianity i.e. 'Coptic Christianity' found in Ethiopean highlands and 'Maronite' Christians' are found in Lebanon.
- The Western Christianity known as Roman Catholic Church sprung in Western and Central Europe. Another branch of Western Christianity is well known as Protestantism or Protestants. Both Catholic and Protestants spread Christianity all over the world.
- After the discovery of America, Western Christianity was carried to America by European migrants and it was modified with number of dimensions. Baptist, Mormon, Lutheran are the examples of the branches of Christianity in North American countries.

Christianity was founded in the first country. A. D. by Jesus of Nazareth. The followers accepted him as 'Christ' a chosen one, sent to fulfil God's promise to Abraham, Issac and Jacob. Bible is the main religious holy book for Christians. Christianity has splits into three branches or three main churches and they are as follows :

(i) The Roman Catholic Church : This is the original Christian Church founded by teaching of Christ. In the 4th century A. D. Christianity became the official religion in Rome. St. Peter who was the Christ's chief disciple propagated it. He was known as Holy father and was recognised as the supreme authority.

(ii) The Eastern Orthodox Church : The Eastern Church Christendom was founded by Constantine, the emperor of eastern Roman empire in 11th century. It consists of Greek, Russian, American and Copic Churches. These Churches have been linked together. There are about 130 million adherents.

(iii)The Protestant Church : This Church of Christianity emerged in the 16th century as a reform activity in Christianity. This Church challenged the corruption and laxity of Roman Pope. Protestant followers appealed for national feelings.

- For example, Lutheranizm Anglicanism arose in England and Calvinism in Switzerland, Holland and Scotland. Protestantism is divided into many denominations. Today the number of Protestant followers is over 200 million.

(B) Islam : Islam as a great monotheistic universalizing faith formed as a result of the teaching of Mohammad Paigambar in the 7th century A. D. Though it was first originated in Western Arabia, but after Mohammad's passing away, Islam made its influence across North Africa and Central Asia.

- Later on the Muslim missionaries with trade connections spread Islamic faith as far South as the Southern Philippines, Indonesian islands and interior China. Turks accepted Islam from the Arab people and carried it through Asia Minor into various parts of South Eastern Europe.
- Islam means submission or total surrender to God. According to Islam, God is absolutely unique, omnipotent, omniscient and

merciful. Men are exhorted to obey his will. The Muslim creed consists of five articles of faith : (i) Belief in God, (ii) in angels, (iii) in Quran, (iv) in the Prophet, and (v) in the day of judgement.

There are two broad divisions within the Muslim community :

(i) The Shias - living in Iran mainly.

(ii) The Sunni - living in Iraq mainly.

- As of 2015 Islam is first with 2.08 billion followers surpassing Christianity. City of Mecca is known as the holiest city of Muslim as it is the birth place of prophet Mohammad. It is well known to Muslim as 'Kaaba - Al - Haram Sharif'.

(C) Hinduism : Hinduism is the oldest religion of India. Hinduism practice polytheism and consequently worship many Gods and Goddesses. However, Brahma is presumed as origin of all Gods. Yoga is the principle teaching of Hinduism that promotes physical and mental discipline, mortification of human body, spiritual peace and happiness. Caste system is the unique character of Hinduism.

- It was originated around 1500 B. C. when the Aryans invaded India. The Aryans were divided into four groups- Brahmins, Kshatriyas, Vaishyas and Shudras. The Brahmins were the priests and hold the top positions. Kshatriyas and Vaishyas and Shudras were warriors and businessmen respectively and they were also relatively privileged. But the fourth Shudras were considered as untouchables and out castes who served the upper castes as slaves.
- The total population of Hindus in 2012 was about 960 million out of which 687 million were in Asia especially in India. There is no central authority in Hinduism and relative importance of shrines is established by tradition not by doctrine. Ved, Geeta, Upanishadas are the holy books of Hinduism. The Hindu holy places comprise a variety of features of the physical environment. Haridwar, Prayagraj Varanasi, Badrinath, Dwarka, Amarnath, Puri, Tirupati are the main places which attract pilgrims from all over the country. The Hindus consider a 'tirtha' as an act of purification. Among the Hindus most of the religious functions are performed at home or at the temple.

(D) Buddhism : Buddhism began in Himalayan foothills of northern India about 500 B. C. It resulted from reform movement within Hinduism that created castes system, untouchability and some orthodox ways of life. Prince Siddhartha founded this religion and he is known as Buddha which means the 'enlightened one'. Shocked as a young man by the inevitability of sickness, old-age and death he renounced his family life in order to wonder as a 'Sramana' or ascetic, in search of religious understanding and a way of release from the human condition.

- Buddha instructed his followers to follow the 'noble eight fold path' i.e. right views, right question, right speech, right conduct, right livelihood, right effort, right mindfulness and concentration. By following these eight noble principles of life one may achieve 'Nirvana'. The state of release from the sufferings of the world. Buddhism first originated in Indian sub-continent and then spread to China and South East Asia. There are two branches of Buddhism : (i) Mahayana Buddhism and (ii) Hinayana Buddhism. Buddhists followers form nearly 6.77% of the total population.

(E) Judaism : Judaism is one of the oldest monotheistic religious group that came into being 400 years ago on the eastern borders of Tigris and Euphrates plains of the Middle East. After its clash with imperial Rome and the destruction of Jerusalem in 70 and 135 A. D. Judaism split into a variety of sub-groups and its followers, the Jews, spread in different parts throughout the world. Jews in Spain and Portugal are known as the Sephardim where as they are well known as Akhkenazim in Central and Eastern Europe. Judaism thus became the system of Jewish religious beliefs, practices and rites.

- The total population of Jews is about 18 million or around 0.4 per cent of the total population of the world. A prominent feature of Judaism is its agricultural calendar which was made by the annual cycle or variation of climatic conditions.

4.3 Distribution of Language and Religions in India

4.3.1 Religion in India

- India is characterised by many religious beliefs and practices. India has no state religion.
- The Indian subcontinent is the birthplace of four of the world's major religions; namely Hinduism, Buddhism, Jainism, and Sikhism.
- According to the 2011 census, 79.8% of the population of India follows Hinduism, 14.2% follows Islam, 2.3% follows Christianity, 1.7% follows Sikhism, and 0.7% follows Buddhism. Zoroastrianism, Sanamahism and Judaism also have an ancient history in India, and each has several thousands of Indian adherents.
- India has the largest population of people following Zoroastrianism (i.e. Parsis and Iranis) and Bahá'í Faith in the world, even though these religions initially originated in Persia. Religion has always been an important part of the country's culture.
- The Constitution of India has declared the right to freedom of religion to be a fundamental right.
- India is home to around 90% of the global population of Hindus. Most Hindu shrines and temples are located in India, as the birthplaces of most Hindu saints.
- Prayagraj hosts the world's largest religious pilgrimage, Prayag Kumbh Mela, where Hindus from across the world come together to bath in the confluence of three sacred rivers of India: the Ganga, the Yamuna, and the Saraswati.
- The Indian diaspora in western countries popularised many aspects of Hindu philosophy such as yoga, meditation, Ayurvedic medicine, divination, karma and reincarnation.
- Several Hindu organisations, such as the Hare Krishna movement, the Brahma Kumaris, the Ananda Marga, and others have spread Indian spiritual beliefs and practices.

- The Indian subcontinent also contains the largest population of Muslims in the world, with about one-third of all Muslims being from South Asia.
- By 2050, the Muslim population of India is projected to grow to 311 million and surpass Indonesia to become the world's largest Muslim population. India is one of the countries in the world with at least 2 million Ahmadi Muslims.
- Evidence attesting to prehistoric religion in the Indian "subcontinent" derives from scattered Mesolithic rock paintings depicting dances and rituals.
- The Harappan people of the Indus Valley Civilisation, (3300 to 1400 BCE) was located on the Indus and Ghaggar-Hakra river valleys, may have worshiped an important mother goddess symbolising fertility and excavations of Indus Valley Civilisation sites show seals with animals and "fire-altars", indicating rituals associated with fire.
- A linga-yoni of a type similar to that which is now worshiped by Hindus has also been found. Hinduism is regarded as the oldest religion in the world, from prehistoric times. Hinduism spread through parts of Southeastern Asia, China, Korea, and Japan. Hindus worship a single god with different forms. The oldest surviving text of Hinduism is the Rigveda, produced during the Vedic period and dating to 1700–1100 BCE. Ramayana and Mahabharata were written approximately from 500–100 BCE. After 200 BCE, several schools of thought were codified in Indian philosophy, including Samkhya, Yoga, Nyaya, Vaisheshika, Purva Mimamsa and Vedanta.

Jainism in India is traced back to 9th century BC with Parshvanatha and his non-violent philosophy.

- Mahavira the 24th Jain Tirthankara (599–527 BCE) stressed five vows, including ahimsa (non-violence) and asteya (non-stealing).
- Gautama Buddha, founded Buddhism, was born to the Shakya clan. His family was native to the plains of Lumbini, in what is now southern Nepal.

- Indian Buddhism peaked during the reign of Ashoka the Great of the Mauryan Empire, who patronised Buddhism. He sent missionaries abroad, allowing Buddhism to spread across Asia.

Bhakti Movement

During the 14–17th BCE, the Bhakti movement swept through Central and Northern India. The Bhakti movement actually started in the eighth-century Tamil south India and gradually spread northwards.. It was initiated by saints. Chaitanya Mahaprabhu, Vallabhacharya, Surdas, Meerabai, Tulsidas, Ravidas, Namdeo, Tukaram and other mystics were some of the saints in the North.

- They taught that people could cast aside the heavy burdens of ritual and caste, and the subtle complexities of philosophy, and simply express their overwhelming love for God.

Sikhism

Guru Nanak (1469–1539) was the founder of Sikhism. The Guru Granth Sahib was first compiled by the fifth Sikh guru, Guru Arjan Dev, from the writings of the first five Sikh gurus and others saints who preached the concept of universal brotherhood, Sikhism strongly rejects the beliefs of fasting (vrata), superstitions, idol worship and circumcsion.

Judaism

Jews began arriving as traders from Judea to the city of Kochi, Kerala, in 562 BCE. More Jews came as exiles from Israel in the year 70 CE, after the destruction of the Second Temple.

Christianity

According to tradition Christianity was first introduced to India by Thomas the Apostle, who visited Muziris in Kerala in 52 CE and the followers are known as Saint Thomas Christians (Syrian Christians or Nasrani) today. There is a general consensus that Christianity was rooted in India by the 6th century AD. Christianity in India has different denominations like Roman Catholicism, Catholicism, Protestantism, Oriental Orthodoxy etc.

- Most Christians reside in South India, particularly in Kerala, Tamil Nadu and Goa. There are also large Christian populations in the North-east Indian states.

Islam

Islam is the second largest religion in India next to Hinduism, with 172 million people identifying as followers of Islam (2011 census). It makes India the country with the largest Muslim population outside Muslim-majority countries. Islam's expansion in India mostly took place under the Delhi Sultanate (1206–1526) and the Mughal Empire (1526–1858), greatly aided by the mystic Sufi tradition.

Demographics

Table 4.7 : Religion in India (2011 Census)

Hinduism	(79.8%)
Islam	(14.2%)
Christianity	(2.3%)
Sikhism	(1.7%)
Buddhism	(0.7%)
Jainism	(0.4%)
Other religions	(0.7%)
Religion not stated	(0.2%)

There are six religions in India which have been awarded "National minority" status-Muslims, Christians, Sikhs, Jains, Buddhists and Zoroastrians.

Table 4.8 : Population trends for major religious groups in India (1951–2011)

Religious group	Population % 1951	Population % 1961	Population % 1971	Population % 1981	Population % 1991	Population % 2001	Population % 2011
Hinduism	84.1%	83.45%	82.73%	82.30%	81.53%	80.46%	79.80%
Islam	9.8%	10.69%	11.21%	11.75%	12.61%	13.43%	14.23%
Christianity	2.30%	2.44%	2.60%	2.44%	2.32%	2.34%	2.30%
Sikhism	1.79%	1.79%	1.89%	1.92%	1.94%	1.87%	1.72%
Buddhism	0.74%	0.74%	0.70%	0.70%	0.77%	0.77%	0.70%
Jainism	0.46%	0.46%	0.48%	0.47%	0.40%	0.41%	0.37%
Zoroastrianism	0.13%	0.09%	0.09%	0.09%	0.08%	0.06%	not counted
Others/ Religion not specified	0.43%	0.43%	0.41%	0.42%	0.44%	0.72%	0.9%

The following is a breakdown of India's religious communities :

Table 4.9 : Characteristics of religious groups.

Religious group	Population (2011) %	Growth (2001-2011)	Sex ratio (2011) (total)	Sex ratio (2011) (rural)	Sex ratio (2011) (urban)	Sex ratio (2011) (child)	Literacy (2011) (%)	Work participation (2011) (%)
Hinduism	79.80%	16.8%	939	946	921	913	73.3%	41.0%
Islam	14.23%	24.6%	951	957	941	943	68.5%	32.6%
Christianity	2.30%	15.5%	1023	1008	1046	958	84.5%	41.9%
Sikhism	1.72%	8.4%	903	905	898	828	75.4%	36.3%
Buddhism	0.70%	6.1%	965	960	973	933	81.3%	43.1%
Jainism	0.37%	5.4%	954	935	959	889	94.9%	35.5%
Others/Religion not specified	0.90%	n/a	959	947	975	974	n/a	n/a

Source : Wikipidia

Rituals

The vast majority of Indians engage in religious rituals on a daily basis. Most Hindus observe religious rituals at home. Observation of rituals vary greatly amongst regions, villages, and individuals. Muslims offer five daily prayers at specific times of the day, indicated by adhan (call to prayer) from the local mosques.

Diet

- India is country with largest vegetarian population. Some Indians practice lacto-vegetarianism. Vegetarianism is less common amongst Sikhs and almost uncommon amongst Muslims, Christians, Bahá'ís, Parsis, and Jews. Jainism requires monks and laity, from all its sects and traditions, to be vegetarian. Occasions like birth, marriage, and death involve what are often elaborate sets of religious customs. Muslims practice a series of life-cycle rituals that differ from those of Hindus, Jains, and Buddhists.

Pilgrimages

- Rumtek Monastery in Sikkim is one of the major tourist attractions of Northeastern India.
- Many Hindu families have their own family patron deity or the kuladevata.
- Hindus worldwide recognise several Indian holy cities, Prayagraj, Haridwar, Varanasi, Ujjain, Rameshwaram and Vrinda van.
- Notable temple cities include Puri, which has a Jagannath temple and Rath Yatra celebration; Tirumala - Tirupati, home

to the Tirumala Venkateswara Temple; and Katra, home to the Vaishno Devi temple.

- Badrinath, Puri, Dwarka and Rameswaram compose the main pilgrimage of Char Dham (four abodes) hosting the four holiest Hindu temples: Badrinath Temple, Jagannath Temple, Dwarkadheesh Temple and Ramanathaswamy Temple respectively.
- The Himalayan towns of Badrinath, Kedarnath, Gangotri, and Yamunotri consists of the smaller Chota Char Dham (mini four abodes) pilgrimage circuit.
- The Kumbh Mela is one of the holiest Hindu pilgrimages that is held every four years.
- Amongst the Eight Great Places of Buddhism, seven are in India. Bodh Gaya, Sarnath and Kushinagar are the places where important events in the life of Gautama Buddha took place.
- For Muslims, the Dargah Shareef of Khwaja Moinuddin Chishti in Ajmer is a major pilgrimage site. Other Islamic pilgrimages include those to the Tomb of Sheikh Salim Chishti in Fatehpur Sikri, Jama Masjid in Delhi, and Haji Ali Dargah in Mumbai.
- Dilwara Temples in Mount Abut, Palitana, Pavapuri, Girnar and Shravanabelagola are notable pilgrimage sites (tirtha) in Jainism.
- The Harmandir Sahib in Amritsar is the most sacred gurdwara of Sikhism.
- The Lotus Temple in Delhi is a prominent house of worship of the Bahá'í faith.
- Relatively new pilgrimage sites include the samadhi of Meher Baba in Meherabad, which is visited by his followers from around the world and the Saibaba temple in Shirdi.

4.3.2 The distribution of Languages in India :

(i) There are several languages in India belonging to different families, the major ones being the Indo-Aryan languages spoken by 78.05% of Indians and Dravidian languages spoken by 19.64%, Southern Indians.

(ii) Other languages spoken by Indians belong to Austro-Asiatic, Tibeto-Burman a few minor language families and 'isolates'.

(iii) The Eighth Schedule of the Indian Constitution lists 22 languages which have been referred to as scheduled languages and given recognitions, status and official encouragement.

(iv) The SIL Ethnologies list 415 living languages in India.

(v) Ethnic groups in India : Indo-Aryan (72%), Dravidian (25%), Mongoloid and others (3%).

(vi) English enjoys the status of subsidiary official language but it is the most important language for national, political and commercial communication.

(vii) Hindi is the most widely spoken language and primary tongue of 41% of the people. There are fourteen other official languages.

Languages in India :

India (780) has the world's second highest number of languages, after Papua New Guinea (839). The Official Language Act, 1963, allowed for the continuation of English language alongside Hindi in the Indian government.

Government of India has also awarded the distinction of *classical language* to Kannada, Malayalam, Odia, Sanskrit, Tamil and Telugu. Clas sical language status is given to languages which have a rich heritage.

According to the Census of India of 2001, India has 122 major languages and 1599 other languages. English continues to be an important language in India. It is used in higher education and in some areas of the Indian government. Hindi, the most commonly spoken language in India today, serves as the *lingua franca* across much of North and Central India.

- Bengali is the second most spoken and understood language in the country with a significant amount of speakers in Eastern and North-eastern regions. The Southern Indian languages are from the Dravidian family of language. The Dravidian languages are indigenous to the Indian subcontinent. The Indo-Aryan languages developed and emerged in three stages — Old Indo-Aryan (1500 BCE to 600 BCE), Middle Indo-Aryan stage (600 BCE and 1000 CE) and New Indo-Aryan (between 1000 CE and 1300 CE).

- Persian, or *Farsi*, was brought to India by the Ghaznavids and other Turko-Afghan dynasties as the court language. In 1837, the British replaced Persian with English and Hindustani in Perso-Arabic script for administrative purposes and the Hindi movement of the 19th Century replaced Persianised vocabulary with Sanskrit derivations.
- Hindustani was strongly influenced by Sanskrit, Arabic and Persian, leading to the emergence of Modern Standard Hindi and Modern Standard Urdu. Bangla language has retained its Sanskritic roots while heavily expanding its vocabulary with words from Persian, English, French and other foreign languages.
- The first official survey of language diversity in the Indian subcontinent was carried out by Sir George Abraham Grierson from 1898 to 1928.
- The People's Linguistic Survey of India recorded over 66 different scripts and more than 780 languages in India
- The People of India (PoI) project of Anthropological Survey of India reported 325 languages which are used for in-group communication by 5,633 Indian communities.
- The Census of India records and publishes data with respect to the number of speakers for languages and dialects, but uses its own unique terminology, distinguishing between *language* and *mother tongue*.

2011 Census

According to 2011 census recognizes 1369 rationalized mother tongues and 1474 names which were treated as 'unclassified' and relegated to 'other' mother tongue category. Out of the 1369 rationalized mother tongues are further grouped into appropriate set 121 languages. In these 121 languages, 22 are already part of the Eighth Schedule to the Constitution of India.

Multilingualism

Table 4.10 : Second and Third languages by number of speakers in India (2011 Census)

Language	First language speakers	First language speakers as a percentage of total population	Second language speakers (millions)	Third language speakers (millions)	Total speakers (millions)[43][44]	Total speakers as a percentage of total population
Hindi	528,347,193	43.63	139	24	692	57.1
English	259,678	0.02	83	46	129	10.6
Bengali	97,237,669	8.30	9	1	107	8.9
Marathi	83,026,680	7.09	13	3	99	8.2
Telugu	81,127,740	6.93	12	1	95	7.8
Tamil	69,026,881	5.89	7	1	77	6.3
Gujarati	55,492,554	4.74	4	1	60	5.0
Urdu	50,772,631	4.34	11	1	63	5.2
Kannada	43,706,512	3.73	14	1	59	4.94
Odia	37,521,324	3.20	5	0.03	43	3.56
Malayalam	34,838,819	2.97	0.05	0.02	36.0	2.9
Punjabi	33,124,726	2.83	0.03	0.003	36.6	3.02
Sanskrit	24,821	0.00185	0.01	0.003	0.025	0.01

Language families

Languages spoken in India belong to several language families, the major ones being the Indo-Aryan languages spoken by 78.05% of Indians and the Dravidian languages spoken by 19.64% of Indians. The most important language families in India are as follows :

Table 4.11

Rank	Language family	Population (2018)
1	Indo-Aryan language family	1,045,000,000 (78.05%)
2	Dravidian language family	265,000,000 (19.64%)
3	Austroasiatic language family	Unknown
4	Sino-Tibetan language family	Unknown
5	Tai–Kadai language family	Unknown
6	Great Andamanese languages	Unknown
Total		**1,340,000,000**

(i) Indo-Aryan language family

It is the largest of the language families in India, in number of speakers. It is a branch of the Indo-Iranian family, subfamily of the Indo-European language family. This language family accounts for some 1035 million speakers, or over 76.5 of the population, as per 2018 estimate.

- The most widely spoken languages of this family are Hindi, Bengali, Marathi, Urdu, Gujarati, Punjabi, Kashmiri, Rajasthani, Sindhi, Assamese (Asamiya), Maithili and Odia. Other Indo-European languages are also spoken in India, the most prominent of which is English.

(ii) Dravidian language family

It is the second largest language family is the Dravidian language family, accounting for some 277 million speakers, or approximately 20.5% as per 2018 estimate. These languages are spoken mainly in southern India and parts of eastern and central India as well as in parts of northeastern Sri Lanka, Pakistan, Nepal and Bangladesh.

The Dravidian languages with the most number of speakers are Tamil, Telugu, Kannada and Malayalam. Dravidian languages are also spoken by small scheduled tribe communities, such as the Oraon and Gond tribes. Only two Dravidian languages are exclusively spoken outside India, Brahui in Pakistan and Dhangar, a dialect of Kurukh, in Nepal.

(iii) Austroasiatic language family

Austroasiatic and numerous small Sino-Tibetan languages, with some 10 and 6 million speakers, respectively, together form 3% of the population. The Austroasiatic language family (*austro* meaning South) has arrived by migration. Austroasiatic languages of mainland India are the Khasi and Munda languages, including Santhali including The languages of the Nicobar islands. With the exceptions of Khasi and Santhali, all Austroasiatic languages are endangered.

(iv) Sino-Tibetan language family

These language family are well represented in India. Sino-Tibetan languages are spoken across the Himalayas in the regions of Ladakh, Himachal Pradesh, Nepal, Sikkim, Bhutan, Arunachal Pradesh, and also in the Indian states of West Bengal, Assam (hills and autonomous councils) Meghalaya, nagaland, Manipur, Tripura and Mizoram. Sino-Tibetan languages spoken in India include the scheduled languages Meitei and Bodo, the non-scheduled languages of Karbi, Lepcha, and many varieties of several related Tibetic, West Himalayish, Tani, Brahmaputran, Angami Pochuri, Tangkhul, Zeme, Kukish Kukish language groups.

(v) Tai-Kadai language family :

Ahom language, had been once the dominant language of the Ahom Kingdom in Assam, but was replaced by the Assamese language (known as Kamrupi. Small Tai communities and their languages are in Assam and Arunachal Pradesh together with Sino-Tibetans, e.g. Tai Phake, Tai Aiton and Tai Khamti.

(vi) Great Andamanese language family

The Great Andamanese languages, consist of a number of extinct, and highly endangered languag. The Ongan family of the southern Andaman Islands, consisting of two extant languages, Önge and Jarawa, and one extinct language, Jangil. Sentinelese, is likely related to the above languages.

(vii) Language isolates

The only language found in the Indian mainland that is considered a language isolate is Nihali. The other language isolates found in the rest of South Asia include Burushaski, a language spoken in Gilgit–Baltistan (administered by Pakistan), Kusunda (in western Nepal) and Vedda (in Sri Lanka). In addition, a Bantu language, Sidi, was spoken until the mid-20th century in Gujarat by the Siddi.

Federal level

Before Independence, English was the sole language used for administrative purposes as well as for higher education. In 1946, the issue of national language was a bitterly contested and members belonging to the northern parts of India insisted that the Constitution be drafted in Hindi with the unofficial translation in English. This was not drafting Committee on the grounds that English was much better to craft the nuanced prose on constitutional subjects. The efforts to make Hindi the pre-eminent language were bitterly resisted by the members from those parts of India where Hindi was not spoken natively.

- Ultimately, a compromise was reached with Hindi in Devanagari script to be the official language of the union but for "fifteen years from the commencement of the Constitution, the English Language shall continue to be used for all the official purposes of the Union for which it was being used immediately before such commencement".

Article 343 (1) of the Constitution of India states "The Official Language of the Union government shall be Hindi in Devanagari script."

- As the date for changeover approached, however, there was much alarm in the non Hindi-speaking areas of India.
- Accordingly, Jawaharlal Nehru ensured the enactment of the Official Languages Act, 1963, which provided that English "may" still be used with Hindi for official purposes, even after 1965.
- In the event, as 1965 approached, India's new Prime Minister Lal Bahadur Shastri prepared to make Hindi paramount with effect from 26 January 1965 which led to widespread agitation. The proposal was dropped, and the Act was amended in 1967 to provide that the use of English would not be ended until a resolution to that effect was passed by the legislature of every state that had not adopted Hindi as its official language, and by each house of the Indian Parliament. Finally Constitution of India does not give any language the status of national language.

Hindi

Hindi, written in Devanagari script is the most prominent language spoken in the country. If not only includes Hindi speakers of Hindustani, but also people who identify as native speakers of related languages who consider their speech to be a dialect of Hindi, the Hindi belt. Hindi (or Hindustani) is the native language of most people living in Delhi, Uttar Pradesh, Uttarakhand, Chhattisgarh, Himachal Pradesh, Chandigarh, Bihar, Jharkhand, Madhya Pradesh, Haryana and Rajasthan.

"Modern Standard Hindi", is one of the official languages of the Union of India. The Rajya Sabha now allows all 22 official languages on the Eighth Schedule to be spoken.

- Hindustani, evolved from '*khari boli*', a prominent tongue of Mughal times, which itself evolved from Apabhraṃśa, an intermediary transition stage from Prakrit, from which the major North Indian Indo-Aryan languages have evolved. Varieties of Hindi spoken in India include Rajasthani, Braj Bhasha, Haryanvi, Bundeli, kannauji, Hindustani,Awadhi, Bagheli, Bhojpuri,Magahi, Nagpuri and Chhattisgarh i. Hindi is taught both as a primary language and language of instruction, and as a second tongue in most states.

English

- English, along with Hindi, is one of the two languages allowed in the Constitution of India for business in Parliament.
- Despite the fact that Hindi has official Government patronage and serves as a *lingua franca* over large parts of India, there was considerable opposition to the use of Hindi in the southern states of India, and English has emerged as a '*de facto lingua franca* ' in India.

Scheduled languages

Till the Twenty-first Amendment of the Constitution of India in 1967, the country recognised 14th official regional languages. The Eighth Schedule of the Constitution of India, as of 1 December 2007, lists 22 languages, which are given in the table below together with the regions where they are used.

Table 4.12 : Schedule Language

Language	Family	Language	Family
Assamese	Indo-Aryan	Malayalam	Dravidian
Bengali (Bangla)	Indo-Aryan	Meitei	Sino-Tibetan
Bodo	Sino-Tibetan	Marathi	Indo-Aryan
Dogri	Indo-Aryan	Nepali	Indo-Aryan
Gujarati	Indo-Aryan	Odia	Indo-Aryan
Hindi	Indo-Aryan	Punjabi	Indo-Aryan
Kannada	Dravidian	Sanskrit	Indo-Aryan
Kashmiri	Indo-Aryan	Santali	Austroasiatic
Konkani	Indo-Aryan	Sindhi	Indo-Aryan
Maithili	Indo-Aryan	Tamil	Dravidian
Urdu	Indo-Aryan	Telugu	Dravidian

- The states, can legislate their own official languages, depending on their linguistic demographics. Certain states having a linguistically defined territory may have only the predominant language in that state as its official language, examples are Karnataka and Gujarat. Telangana, with a sizeable Urdu-speaking Muslim population, has two languages, Telugu and Urdu, as its official languages. Jammu and Kashmir uses Urdu, which is spoken by fewer than 1% of the population.

- Meghalaya uses English spoken by 0.01% of the population. It has turned majority languages into "minority languages" in a functional sense.

Lists of Official Languages of States and Union Territories of India

- In addition to states and union territories, India has autonomous administrative regions which may be permitted to select their own official language i.e. the Bodo language. Assamese and English in Bodoland and Bengali in the Barak Valley as its official languages.

Main languages of India

Regional languages

- During British India, English was the only language used for administrative purposes as well as for higher education purposes. When India became independent in 1947, the Indian legislators had the following choices available:

(i) Making "Hindi", which a plurality of the people (41%) identified as their native language, the official language.

(ii) Making English, as preferred by non-Hindi speakers, particularly Kannadigas and Tamils, and those from Mizoram and Nagaland etc.

(iii) Declare both Hindi and English as official languages and each state is given freedom to choose the official language of the state.

Bengali

The Bengal region, consists of the nation of Bangladesh and the states of West Bengal, Tripura and Barak Valley region of Assam. Bengali is the sixth most spoken language in the world. After the partition of India (1947), refugees from East Pakistan were settled in Tripura, and Jharkhand and the union territory of Andaman and Nicobar, Maharashtra and Gujarat. Bengali language developed from Abahatta, a derivative of Apabhramsha, itself derived from Magadhi Prakrit.

- The modern Bengali vocabulary contains the vocabulary base from Magadhi Prakrit and Pali, Sanskrit, Persian, Arabic, Austroasiatic languages and other languages. Bengali language has developed a rich cultural base spanning art, music, literature and religion. Bengali has some of the oldest literature of all modern Indo-Aryan languages, dating from about 10th to 12th century. UNESCO declared in 1999 as the International Mother Language Day in commemoration of the Bengali Language Movement in 1952.

Marathi

Marathi is an Indo-Aryan language. It is the official language and co-official language in Maharashtra and Goa respectively, and is one of the official languages of India. Marathi has the third largest number of native speakers in India. Marathi has some of the oldest literature of all modern Indo-Aryan languages, dating from about 1200 AD. The major dialects of Marathi are Standard Marathi and the Varhadi dialect. There are other related languages such as Khandeshi, Dangi, Vadvali and Samavedi. Malvani Konkani has been heavily influenced by Marathi varieties. Marathi is one of several languages that descend from Maharashtri Prakrit.

- Marathi is the official language of Maharashtra and co-official language in the union territories of Daman and Diu and Dadra and Nagar Haveli. The primary influence of Prakrit, Maharashtri, Dravidian languages, Apabhraṃśa and Sanskrit is obvious. At least 50% of the words in Marathi are either taken or derived from Sanskrit.

Telugu

Telugu is an important Dravidian language in India and around the world. Telugu is an official language in Andhra Pradesh, Telangana and Yanam. It is also spoken by many people in the Andaman and Nicobar Islands, Chhattisgarh, Karnataka, Maharashtra, Odisha, Tamil Nadu, Gujarat and by the Gypsy people in Shi Lanka. It is one of six languages with classical status in India.

- Telugu ranks fourth by the number of native speakers in India fifteenth in the *Ethnologue* list of most-spoken languages worldwide and is the most widely spoken Dravidian language.

Tamil

- Tamil is a Dravidian language mainly spoken in Tamil Nadu, Puducherry and many parts of Sri Lanka, minorities in the Andaman and Nicobar Islands, Kerala, Karnataka, Andhra Pradesh, Malaysia, Singapore, Mauritius and throughout the world.
- Tamil ranks fifth by the number of native speakers in India and ranks 20th in the list of most spoken languages. It is one of the 22 scheduled languages of India and was the first Indian language to be declared a classical language by the Government of India. It has been described as "the only language of contemporary India which is recognisably continuous with a classical past." It is also recognized as a minority language in Canada, Malaysia, Mauritius and South Africa.

Urdu

- After independence, Modern Standard Urdu, became the national language of Pakistan. Hindustani was made the second language of British Indian Empire after English and considered as the language of administration. Urdu along with Hindi, is one of the 22 officially recognised regional languages of India and also an official language in the Indian states of Jammu and Kashmir, Delhi, Uttar Pradesh, Bihar and Telangana that have significant Muslim populations.

Gujarati

- Gujarati is an Indo-Aryan language, native to the west Indian region of Gujarat. Gujarati is part of the greater Indo-European language family. Gujarati (i) from Old Gujarati, the same source as that of Rajasthani. Gujarati is the chief language in the Indian state of Gujarat. It is also an official language in the union territories of Daman and Diu and Dadra and Nagar Haveli.

Kannada

- Kannada language is a Dravidian language. The earliest written records are from the 5th century, and the earliest available literature in rich manuscript (*Kavirajamarga*) is from. 850. Kannada language has the second oldest written tradition of all languages of India, making Karnataka state "one of the most densely inscribed pieces of real estate in the world". According to Garg and Shipely, more than a thousand notable writers have contributed to the wealth of the language.

Malayalam

- Malayalam has official language status in the state of Kerala and in the union territories of Lakshadweep and Puducherry. It belongs to the Dravidian family of languages. Malayalam is also spoken in the neighboring states of Tamil Nadu and Karnataka; with some speakers in the Nilgiris, Kanyakumari and Coimbatore districts of Tamil Nadu, and the Dakshina Kannada and the Kodagu district of Karnataka. Malayalam originated from Middle Tamil (Sen-Tamil) in the 7th century.

Odia

Odia is primarily spoken in the Indian state of Odisha. It was declared as a classical language of India in 2014. Odia is thought to have originated from Udra Prakrit similar to Udra Magadhi, a language spoken in eastern India over 2,500 years ago. The National Manuscripts Mission of India have found around 213,000 unearthed and preserved manuscripts written in Odia.

Punjabi

Punjabi, written in the Gurmukhi script in India, is one of the prominent languages of India. In Pakistan it is written in the Shahmukhi alphabet. It is mainly spoken in Punjab but also in neighboring areas. It is an official language of Delhi and Punjab.

Assamese

Asamiya or Assamese language is most popular in the state of Assam and Brahmaputra Valley. It's an Eastern Indo-Aryan language.

Maithili

Maithili is an Indo-Aryan language spoken in the Bihar and Jharkhand states of India, eastern Terai, of Nepal, and it is the second mot prevalent language of Nepal. Today it is written in the Devanagari script. In 2003, Maithili was included in the Eighth Schedule of the Indian Constitution as a recognised regional language of India.

Classical Language

Several languages were granted the Classical status, and demands have been made for other languages.

Languages thus far declared to be Classical are as follows :

- Tamil (in 2004),

- Sanskrit (in 2005),
- Kannada (in 2008),
- Telugu (in 2008),
- Malayalam (in 2013)
- Odia (in 2014).

Other local languages and dialects

The 2001 census identified the following native languages having more than one million speakers. Most of them are dialects/variants grouped under Hindi.

Table 4.13 : Other Local Languages

Languages	No. of native speakers	Languages	No. of native speakers
Bhojpuri	33,099,497	Laman/Lambadi	2,707,562
Rajasthani	18,355,613	Awadhi	2,529,308
Magadhi/Magahi	13,978,565	Harauti	2,462,867
Chhattisgarhi	13,260,186	Garhwali	2,267,314
Haryanvi	7,997,192	Nimadi	2,148,146
Marwari	7,936,183	Sadan/Sadri	2,044,776
Malvi	5,565,167	Kumauni	2,003,783
Mewari	5,091,697	Dhundhari	1,871,130
Khorth/Khotta	4,725,927	Tulu	1,722,768
Bundeli	3,072,147	Surgujia	1,458,533
Bagheli	2,865,011	Bagri Rajasthani	1,434,123
Pahari	2,832,825	Banjari	1,259,821
Surajpuri	1,217,019	Nagpuria	1,242,586
Kangri	1,122,843		

- India has several languages in use; choosing any single language as an official language presents problems to all those whose "mother tongue" is different. Local official language commissions have been established and various steps are being taken in a direction to reduce tensions and friction.
- The first major linguistic conflict, known as the Anti-Hindi agitations of Tamil Nadu, took place in Tamil Nadu against the implementation of Hindi as the official language of India.

- Strong cultural pride based on language is also found in other Indian states such as Karnataka, West Bengal, Punjab and Maharashtra.
- The GOI attempts to assuage these conflicts with various campaigns, coordinated by the Central Institute of Indian Languages, Mysore, a branch of the Department of Higher Education, Language Bureau, and the Ministry of Human Resource Development.
- Most languages in India are written in Brahmi-derived scripts, such as Devanagari, Tamil, Telugu, Kannada, Meitei Mayek, Odia, Eastern Nagari - Assamese/Bengali, etc., though Urdu is written in a script derived from Arabic, and a few minor languages such as Santali use independent scripts.
- Hindi, Marathi, Maithili and Angika are written using the Devanagari Script. Most major languages are written using a script specific to them, such as Assamese with Asamiya, Bengal with Bengali, Punjabi with Gurmukhi, Meitei with Meitei. Mayek, Odia with Odiascript, Gurarati with Gujarati, etc. Urdu and sometimes Kashmiri, Saraiki and Sindhi are written in modified versions of the Perso-Arabic script.

POINTS TO REMEMBER

- Language is what people use to communicate with each other.
- There are about 7000 languages spoken in the world today.
- A world language is one that is spoken internationally and learned and spoken by numerous people as second language.

(I) Asian languages : (i) Arabic, (ii) Chinese, (iii) Persian, (iv) Indian language.

(II) European languages : (i) English, (ii) French, (iii) German, (iv) Russian, (v) Spanish.

- **Major language families in** the **world :** (i) Indo-European, (ii) Germani, (iii) Romanie (iv) Balto-Slavic, (v) Indo-Iranian, (vi) Sino-Tibetan, (vii) Semito-Hametic, (viii) African, (ix) Others,
- Largest Religions : Christianity, Islam, Hinduism, Buddhism, etc.

- **Major Religions groups :** Christianity, Islam, Hinduism, Buddhism, Judaism etc.
- Indo Aryan language family is the largest in India.
- The second largest language family is the Dravidian language family.
- **Language families in India :** (i) Indo-Aryan, (ii) Dravidian, (iii) Anstoasiatic, (iv) Sino-Tibetan, (v) Tai Kadai, (vi) Great Andamanese, (vii) Language Isolates.
- **Language in India :** Hindi, Bengali, Marathi, Telugu, Tamil, Gujarati, Kannada, Malayalam, Udia, Punjabi, Assamese, Maithili etc.

✧ QUESTIONS ✧

Q. I : Answer the following questions in detail.

(1) Define language. What are the world languages ?

(2) What are the major language families in the world ?

(3) What are the major Religion groups in the world ?

(4) What are the main Religions in India ?

(5) Write in detail about the languages in India.

(6) What are the language families in India ?

(7) What are the official languages of states and union territories in India ?

Q. II : Write short notes :

(1) The Indo-European language family.

(2) Middle-Eastern Religions.

(3) Indo-Aryan and Dravadian language family

(4) Dravidian language family.

(5) Regional language in India.

(6) Classification of Religion.

(7) Religions in India.

(8) Distribution of Language.

(9) Pilgrimage centres in India.

❋ ❋ ❋